THE LAST DAYS

Steven Spielberg and
Survivors of the Shoah Visual History Foundation

THE LAST DAYS

With an Introduction
by David Cesarani

St. Martin's Press　New York

A Thomas Dunne Book
An imprint of St. Martin's Press
First US edition published in 1999
10 9 8 7 6 5 4 3 2 1
First published in Great Britain in 1999 by Weidenfeld & Nicolson

Historical Consultants
Dr Michael Berenbaum, Dr Randolph Braham

Editorial & Creative Consultants
June Beallor and James Moll

Associate Editor
Aaron Zarrow

Designed by Design Revolution
Printed and Bound in Italy
A CIP catalogue record for this book is
available from the British Library
ISBN 0-312-20462-0

SURVIVORS OF THE
S H O A H
VISUAL HISTORY FOUNDATION

Design and layout by Weidenfeld & Nicolson, 1999

This publication was generously supported by the
SARA LEE FOUNDATION

STEVEN SPIELBERG AND THE SHOAH FOUNDATION PRESENT A KEN LIPPER/JUNE BEALLOR PRODUCTION
"THE LAST DAYS" A FILM BY JAMES MOLL MUSIC BY HANS ZIMMER DIRECTOR OF PHOTOGRAPHY HARRIS DONE
ASSOCIATE EDITORS MAJA VRVILO RICHARD KREITMAN ASSOCIATE PRODUCERS ELYSE KATZ AARON ZARROW EXECUTIVE PRODUCER STEVEN SPIELBERG
PG-13 PARENTS STRONGLY CAUTIONED Some Material May Be Inappropriate for Children Under 13   DOLBY STEREO®   PRODUCED BY JUNE BEALLOR KEN LIPPER DIRECTED AND EDITED BY JAMES MOLL OCTOBER FILMS
©1998 Survivors of the Shoah Visual History Foundation. The Shoah Foundation and Survivors of the Shoah Visual History Foundation are trademarks/servicemarks of Survivors of the Shoah Visual History Foundation. Artwork ©1998 October Films, Inc. www.octoberfilms.com

The Last Days film was made possible by a grant from the Kenneth and Evelyn Lipper Foundation

Contents

PREFACE

STEVEN SPIELBERG

This book expands upon *The Last Days* film, a journey tracing the experiences of five courageous Hungarian Holocaust survivors – Alice Lok Cahana, Irene Zisblatt, Tom Lantos, Renée Firestone and Bill Basch. Their individual stories of survival and regeneration are remarkable, and I am extremely proud to know these people. They represent an important milestone for me in my own journey, which began in the fall of 1993 as I was filming *Schindler's List*.

As we struggled to tell the story of the Schindler Jews against the backdrop of hatred, persecution and death, filming took on extraordinary meaning. While we did not want to dishonour the victims of the Holocaust by making a dramatic film within the concentration camp grounds, we did work just outside the gates. Our sense of what we were trying to accomplish

became even more profound on the days when survivors of the Holocaust came to the set to see what we were doing, to support us and to share their own experiences.

Many of the survivors who visited us shared their experiences for the first time. They felt forgotten, as if the world did not want to know or deal with them. Each person made an impression on me, and profoundly affected the making of *Schindler's List*.

On the plane home, I reflected on this experience and was inspired to establish Survivors of the Shoah Visual History Foundation, to welcome Holocaust survivors and offer an opportunity for them to give videotaped testimony of their experiences. The resulting collection of testimonies would be used for Holocaust and tolerance education and as a research tool for scholars and historians for generations to come.

My hope was for students of this and future generations to have the same experience I did – to see the faces and hear the voices of these eye-witnesses to history. Who could better convey the events that took place?

The Last Days is the third documentary from the Foundation, and the first to be released in theatres worldwide. It follows five Hungarians who fell victim to Adolf Hitler's final genocidal push at the end of the Second World War. The survivors' accounts are personal, revealing and difficult. Bill Basch questions 'Why did I survive? Why did God spare me?'

It is clear from these powerful testimonies that the survivors of the Holocaust indeed share a purpose – to tell their stories.

Steven Spielberg
Founder and Chairman, Survivors of the Shoah Visual History Foundation

PROLOGUE

MICHAEL BERENBAUM

In 1994 Steven Spielberg founded Survivors of the Shoah Visual History Foundation with an urgent mission: to record the testimonies of Holocaust survivors, bystanders and eyewitnesses, liberators and rescuers before it was too late.

It was a race against time.

Survivors were rapidly aging, within a few years, the last eyewitnesses would be gone.

It was the right time.

Just after the war, many survivors were anxious to tell the world about their experience, their tragedy. They were silenced by disbelief or incredulity. In mid-life, many wanted to share with their children, but they were afraid of disquieting them.

They had made two commitments to those they left behind. 'Remember,' they pledged. 'Do not let the world forget.'

Now, before it is too late, they were invited to ensure that their stories will be preserved. They understood that it was now or never. The memory would have to be shared if it was to go forth into the future.

Now was the time.

Schindler's List and Holocaust museums had heightened interest in the Event. The significance of the Holocaust was intensifying the more distant we grew from the event. In classrooms throughout the world, the encounter between survivors and children had become electrifying, the transmission of memory, a discussion of values, a warning against prejudice, antisemitism, racism and indifference.

So the work of the Foundation began in order that generations will remember what so few lived to tell.

The results have been impressive. By the

close of 1998 50,000 testimonies have been gathered in 31 languages in 57 countries. More than 114,000 hours of testimony, enough tape to circumnavigate the globe. It would take a person more than thirteen years and six months to view the entire collection, working 24 hours a day, seven days a week.

The task of the Foundation is to gather, to catalogue and to disseminate the testimonies to as many remote sites as technology and budget will permit.

All in the service of education.

The Last Days, the film and the book, is one of the initial projects of the Foundation's forays into education. The film portrays the last year of World War II and the accelerated programme of the destruction of Hungarian Jewry using the narrative voices of five survivors; Renée Firestone, Alice Lok Cahana, Tom Lantos, Bill Basch and Irene Zisblatt.

A word about that last year.

We tend to see the Holocaust as a monolith, but in actuality the fate of Jews during the Holocaust differed country by country. In Germany, the annihilation of the Jews took twelve years from the Nazi rise to power in 1933 to the end of the Third Reich in 1945. Jews were defined, their assets confiscated and they were deported to the east, where many were killed. The first two stages took some eight years, deportation and death took two years. In Poland, the process repeated itself but a new stage was introduced. Definition to expropriation followed by two to four years of ghettoization and then deportation to death.

In Hungary the entire process took less than four months. The Germans invaded in March 1944. Jews were defined immediately and their property was confiscated, by May most Hungarian Jews were ghettoized; on 15 May, the deportation began and by 8 July almost 440,000 Jews were deported to Auschwitz. By 9 July, the date of Raoul Wallenberg's arrival in Budapest, the Jews of Budapest were the last Jews in a country that everywhere else had become *Judenrein* (free of Jews) in just 54 days.

Prior to the deportation of Jews from Hungarian territory, Auschwitz had been but one of six death camps established by the Germans in occupied Poland. It had been no more lethal than Belzec and less murderous than Treblinka, two of the *Aktion* Reinhard killing centres established in the spring of 1942. But during seven weeks of daily transports from each of the regions of Hungary, Auschwitz overtook the other camps and became the epicenter of the killing process.

What makes the fate of Hungarian Jewry so difficult to fathom is that the destruction took place in 1944, two years after the establishment of the death camps and well after the murder of most of European Jewry. By the spring of 1944, it was clear that Germany would lose the war. Their defeat was only a matter of time. Allied leaders had valid and accurate information about the scope of the killings and general knowledge of their location. Hungarian Jewish leaders could have known, and perhaps should have known, what was happening. There is reason to believe that they had been informed of what was happening elsewhere, of what was about to happen to them – and still no warnings were issued. Little was done, less was accomplished.

Because of the killing of Hungarian Jews, requests were forwarded to Allied leaders to bomb Auschwitz, appeals were made by the Vatican, by neutral leaders, by the king of Sweden to Horthy, the Hungarian head of state; thus, intensifying our fascination with this most intense chapter of the "Final Solution". Still the killing proceeded at a ferocious pace without parallel in the Holocaust.

Those who survived the initial *selektion* were young and able bodied. They worked in the slave labour camp of Auschwitz called Buna-Monowitz. When the Russians approached Auschwitz, they faced another arduous journey, the death marches of January 1945. They were forced to walk hundreds of miles in the dead of the Polish winter, to push beyond human endurance.

The film, *The Last Days*, does what a visual medium can do. It presents the face and voice of the survivor, narrating his/her experiences. It begins when the world was whole and it takes us through each stage of the Holocaust and the survivors' return to the towns of their birth and the camp of their incarceration, some fifty two years after liberation. Brilliantly directed and edited by James Moll and produced by Kenneth Lipper and June Beallor, the film demonstrates the power and the simplicity of the narrative voice.

Yet the film grows in importance as this book presents the experience in its full historical context. Survivors' narratives are sandwiched between a fine historical introduction by David Cesarani, a distinguished Israeli historian, and an epilogue by Randolph Braham, the Dean of historians of the Holocaust in Hungary and himself a survivor. Cesarani's assignment was not easy: to write a detailed but general history of Hungarian Jewry that permits the non-specialist to understand, in full, the historical context of their destruction. Braham is featured in the film. His epilogue is a moving work that is at once historical and personal. And each of the survivors is given the opportunity to tell their story.

Read their narratives, understand their situations, grapple with their dilemmas and share, but for a moment, their anguish and their struggle. They are but five of the more than 50,000 the Foundation has recorded. Look and listen and you will glimpse the power of what is contained in the Foundation's archive.

And remember, they are the survivors. For every one we have interviewed, 120 were left behind, killed in the nearly successful "Final Solution of the Jewish problem" as the Nazis euphemistically called it. Those who were left behind were denied their name and their identity. They were nameless and faceless. The survivors are not.

It is five minutes to midnight in the life of the survivors, but it is early morning in our efforts to understand the Holocaust and to learn what must be learned from the past to reshape our tomorrow. We are proud of this poignant and powerful presentation of the past.

Michael Berenbaum
President, Survivors of the Shoah Visual History Foundation, Los Angeles, California.

MODERN EUROPE WITH HISTORICAL GERMAN AND HUNGARIAN BORDERS

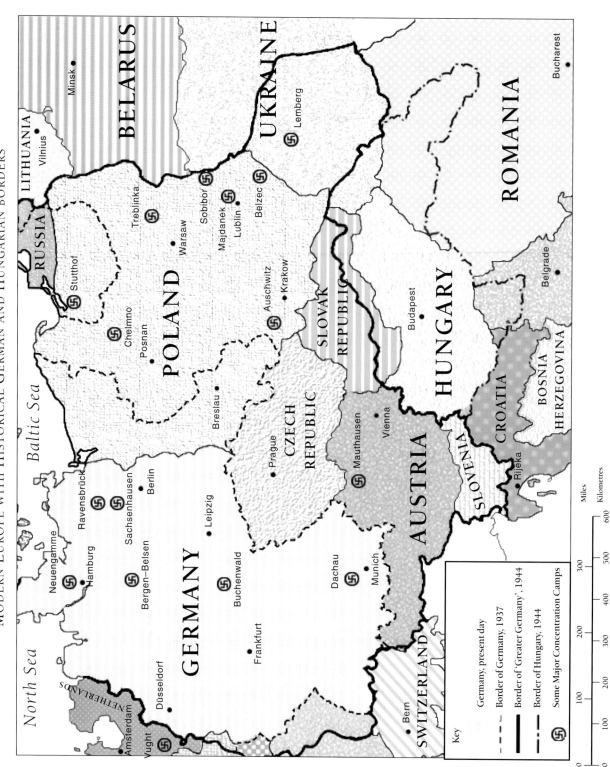

Key

Germany, present day

- - - Border of Germany, 1937

—— Border of 'Greater Germany', 1944

—·—·— Border of Hungary, 1944

Ⓢ Some Major Concentration Camps

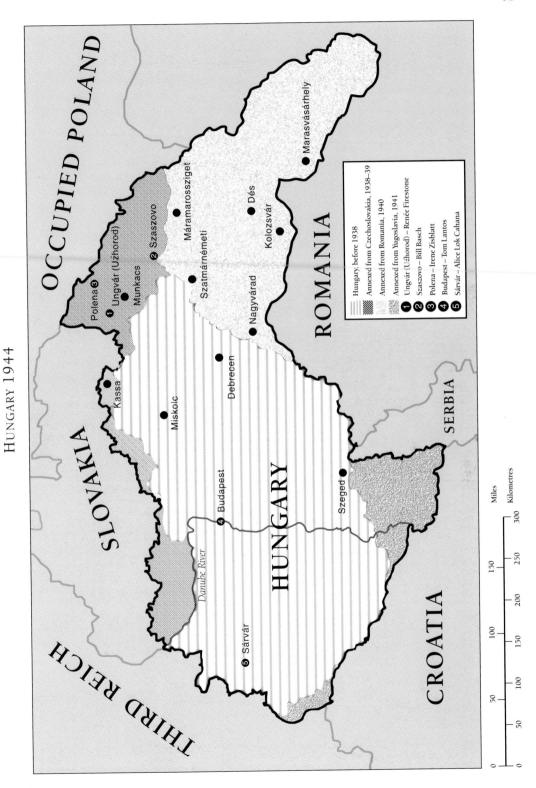

HUNGARY 1944

THIRD REICH

SLOVAKIA

OCCUPIED POLAND

ROMANIA

SERBIA

CROATIA

HUNGARY

Kassa
Miskolc
Debrecen
Budapest ④
Szeged
Sárvár ⑤
Danube River

Polena ③
Ungvár (Uzhorod) ①
Munkács
Szaszovo ②
Máramarossziget
Szatmárnémeti
Nagyvárad
Dés
Kolozsvár
Marasvásárhely

Hungary, before 1938
Annexed from Czechoslovakia, 1938–39
Annexed from Romania, 1940
Annexed from Yugoslavia, 1941
① Ungvár (Uzhorod) – Renée Firestone
② Szaszovo – Bill Basch
③ Polena – Irene Zisblatt
④ Budapest – Tom Lantos
⑤ Sárvár – Alice Lok Cahana

Miles
0   50   100   150   300
Kilometres
0   50   150   200   250   300

13

INTRODUCTION

DAVID CESARANI

I

A Jewish presence in Hungary dates back to Roman times. What was destroyed by the Nazis in a few months in 1944–5 was a singular part of Jewish civilization that had flowered in a unique conjunction with Magyar history over many centuries. Although this volume concentrates on the years of crisis and devastation, it should never be forgotten that the individual stories are threads in a rich weave that stretches back hundreds of years.

The Hungarian Jewish community of modern times dates back to the late seventeenth century after the Ottoman Turks, who had conquered Hungary in 1526, were driven out by the Austrian Habsburgs. The Turks encouraged Jews to settle in the countryside, and in towns and cities in return for paying high taxes and performing useful economic tasks. These settlers, who came mainly from the provinces of Bohemia and Moravia, were the pioneers of modern Hungarian Jewry.

During the seventeenth century the Jewish population increased from 15,000 to around 80,000. By 1805 the number of Jews stood at about 130,000. They were chiefly engaged in trade and commerce, but they made a special contribution to the development of manufacturing. Despite outbreaks of antisemitism, the influence of the Enlightenment tended to improve their position. In an attempt to modernise the outlook of the Jews and their social-economic structure, Joseph II of Austria (r. 1780–90) freed them of many burdensome restrictions, but also obliged them to shed aspects of Jewish tradition. Most Jews embraced this reciprocal arrangement and eagerly entered the professions and the arts. In the nineteenth century Jews played a leading role in the industrialization of Hungary and

The Hungarian Gendarmerie, eventually the major instrument of state power in the ghettoisation and deportation of 440,000 Jews

Frontier piece: German youth salutes Hitler.

transformed the financial services sector along with the distributive trades.

As their prosperity grew the Jews began to demand an end to discrimination based on religious grounds. Although many Hungarian patriots who wanted to create a modern, free Hungary supported them, the Jews had to wait till 1867 and the establishment of Hungarian autonomy within the Habsburg Empire before they gained full equality. Even then it was expected that the Jews would prove that they 'deserved' to be full citizens. Amongst Hungarian Jews it became received wisdom that their status rested on conspicuous patriotism and service to the state. Religious reformers fought to make Judaism appear more acceptable to the Christian majority, a move which divided the Jewish population into antagonistic camps. The split between Orthodox Jews and the Neolog (reform) Jews gravely weakened Hungarian Jewry in times of crisis.

Trouble was not slow in coming. The fantastic growth in Jewish population from 130,000 at the start of the nineteenth century to 625,000 by 1880, peaking at 915,000 in 1910 (or 5 per cent of all Hungarians) alarmed some Christian Magyar nationalists. The burgeoning numbers and influence of the Jews was most pronounced in Budapest itself. There the Jewish population expanded from just

1,734 in 1825, to 17,000 in 1850, 45,000 in 1870, reaching 104,000 in 1890. At this point Jews formed around 20 per cent of the city's total population. In 1910 the Jewish population of Budapest reached 204,000 or just over 23 per cent of the capital's denizens (and represented 22 per cent of all of Hungarian Jewry).

By 1910, Jews comprised 40 per cent of all those employed in commerce, finance and the professions. Jews owned or ran the largest industrial concerns. Having won access to higher education they flooded into the free professions: they numbered 55 per cent of lawyers, 40 per cent of doctors, 35 per cent of journalists in Hungary. This concentration was even more marked in Budapest where, by 1910, Jews comprised 52 per cent of all industrial employers, 64 per cent of all those engaged in trade and finance, 61 per cent of all lawyers and 59 per cent of all doctors.

The migration of Jews from the rural lands in the north and east to the towns and cities caused fear and resentment. In April 1875 Győző Istóczy (1842–1915), a member of parliament, protested that the Jews were too numerous and too powerful in Hungary. Despite being granted equality they didn't act like other citizens and preserved their separateness. The constant arrival of more 'Eastern Jews' was seen as a threat to Christians and Hungarian identity.

Christian Magyars were happy to stand back in admiration as Jewish entrepreneurship brought prosperity to their country. However, when inflation drove up the prices of manufactured goods faster than the cost of agricultural produce, the gentry found their real incomes falling. When their offspring had to seek employment in the state bureaucracy or the professions they encountered Jews as rivals. The gentry started to blame Jewish 'domination' of the economy for their woes and Istóczy soon became their champion. In October 1883 the Antisemitic Party was founded explicitly to 'protect' Christian businessmen, artisans and farmers from the Jews.

The close of the era of harmonious relations between Jews and Christians in Hungary was symbolised by revival of the myth that Jews committed ritual murder against Christians. In April 1882 a young girl disappeared from the small town of Tiszaeszlár, to the north-east of Budapest. The local Catholic priest maintained that the Jews were to blame. His insinuations were taken up by the Catholic press and echoed by Istóczy. Several Jews were subsequently arrested and a state prosecutor appointed to investigate. After a three-month trial the defendants were found not guilty, but the damage was done. The verdict triggered anti-Jewish violence

all over Hungary; troops had to be brought into the capital to quell the disturbances.

In the general election of 1884 Istoczy's Antisemitic Party won seventeen seats. Even though its representation in Parliament subsequently declined, it was a constant source of antisemitic agitation and abuse. In 1892 the Catholic Church promoted the formation of the Catholic People's Party, which shared many of Istóczy's prejudices. One of its patrons, Bishop Ottokár Prohászka, pronounced that 'The Jewish cancer has eaten at the Christian Hungarian nation everywhere.'

From the 1890s antisemitism put down deep roots in Hungary. The gentry, disillusioned with modernization and economic change, turned on the Jews, whom they identified with every undesirable aspect of progress. Students and professionals who found themselves competing with the Jews complained that there were too many Jews in 'their' country. To justify calls for the renewed exclusion of the Jews, Hungarian ultra-nationalists characterised them as racial as well as religious outsiders who could never become 'true Magyars'. Defeat and territorial losses in World War I (1914–18) transformed this antisemitism from an important, if marginal, strand of Hungarian politics into one of its central features.

At the beginning of October 1918 the

Hungarian government approached the United States seeking peace terms with the Allied powers. Meanwhile the Czechs, Slovaks, Croats, and Ruthenians threw off rule from Budapest and Vienna. A revolution in Budapest led to the appointment of a liberal democratic government under Count Mihály Károlyi (1875–1955). An armistice was proclaimed on 3 November 1918 and Hungary became an independent republic, but the momentum for radical change could not be halted. In March 1919 Károlyi's government fell and in its place Béla Kun took power at the head of a Soviet-style regime.

Kun (1886–1939) came from a Jewish family in Transylvania. He received a general education and became active in the left-wing Social Democrats. In 1916, while serving in the army, he was captured on the Russian front and sent to a POW camp. There he encountered Bolshevik propaganda and became a Communist. He returned to his native land in November 1918 and leapt into revolutionary activity. Kun and the Communists manœuvred themselves into leadership of the workers and soldiers councils which held power on the streets and declared Hungary a Soviet Republic.

From the outset of the revolution, leftists of Jewish origin were associated with radical change. Several leading ministers of Károlyi's government were Jewish. No less than eighteen out of twenty-nine members of Kun's Revolutionary-Ruling Council were Jews. The number of Jews who were active at a local level in government agencies, the police or the revolutionary militia was large. There were several reasons for this preponderance. The radicals were mainly drawn from the intelligentsia and Jews were greatly over represented amongst the educated elite. The revolution promised to end the discrimination and prejudice from which they had suffered. For them the vision of a society in which ethnicity, nationalism or religion counted for nothing was especially attractive.

The Communist regime did not last for long. Hungarian counter-revolutionaries, led by Admiral Miklós Horthy (1868–1957), gathered in Szeged, plotted its downfall. In April 1919 a Romanian Army invaded Hungary in order to suppress the revolution while Horthy's 'Hungarian National Army' proceeded to crush the Soviets, town by town. It was assisted by a horde of underground, ultra-patriotic and anti-Communist secret societies. The army and the societies were all rabidly antisemitic, but in an ominous development anti-Jewish feeling spread even more widely.

The leaders and organisations of every Christian denomination gave their blessing to the counter-revolution against atheistic Communism. Hungarian nationalism, Christian anti-Judaism, anti-Communism and antisemitism mingled explosively. Wherever the Hungarian National Army and the secret societies operated Jews were murdered and tortured. After the Romanian forces occupied Budapest in early August and helped install a right-wing government under Horthy, who assumed the title of Regent, a reign of counter-revolutionary terror was initiated across the entire country. Over 200 Jews died in a series of bloody pogroms between August and November 1919.

During the worst of the 'White Terror', as this period was called, some young Jews, mainly students, banded together to form self-defence units in Budapest. The universities became the next target for the antisemitic, counter-revolutionary government.

Since so many of the revolutionaries had been Jews and since so many of them were intellectuals antisemites concluded that the universities were the breeding ground for 'Jewish-Bolshevism'. The new Prime Minister, Pál Teleki (1879–1941), proposed a law to ban anyone who was active in the revolutionary movements from attending university and to limit the number of Jews to six per cent of the total student body, roughly the percentage of the Jews in the Hungarian population. The law to impose a *numerus clausus*, or quota, on the Jews was welcomed by the universities. At Budapest's Catholic University the faculty had ostentatiously shown sympathy for Christian students who assaulted Jewish students and demanded limits to the number of Jews allowed to enter higher education. Despite Jewish protests, in September 1920 the law was passed. Its effect was dramatic. From 4,288 Jewish students at the University of Budapest in 1918 the number fell to 459 in 1921. Thousands of young Jews were forced to study abroad.

Hungary's Jews continued to oppose this blatant act of discrimination and worked with parliamentary allies in the Social Democratic Party and the Liberal Party for its repeal. But their efforts only stimulated more anti-Jewish student riots led by Gyula Gömbös (1886–1936), who would later emerge as a powerful political figure and dyed-in-the-wool antisemite. A change to the law in December 1925, ostensibly to exempt the children of Hungarian Jewish war veterans, actually made the discrimination worse: by exempting one segment of the Jewish population from discrimination without increasing the overall quota it diminished the number of places available to all the rest.

The territorial losses which Hungary suffered under the Treaty of Trianon in 1920 had fundamentally and adversely affected the position of the Jews. While Hungary was a multi-national empire, with about ten million Hungarians ruling over a population of assorted nationalities that numbered as many, the Jews who were enthusiastic Magyarisers were valuable allies. Their economic skills made them even more highly prized. But once Hungary had been reduced to a virtually homogeneous Magyar rump the Jews were the only large ethnic minority. Their domination of sections of society and the economy then stood out like a sore thumb and their efforts to assimilate aroused only resentment. With the loss of its colonial holdings, thousands of officers and civil servants lost their jobs; the career opportunities for Hungarians shrank. Not only were the Jews not needed, it now seemed that they actually stood in the way of the 'real' Hungarians.

Antisemitism permeated society. A host of professional bodies took their cue from the *numerus clausus* and either banned Jews or limited their numbers. Social and sports clubs, including the famous 'casinos', which were at the heart of Hungarian high society, excluded Jewish members. To most

Christian Hungarians the ideal of assimilation had had its day.

Throughout the 1920s and 1930s antisemitism continued to disfigure Hungarian political life. Gyula Gömbös forged links with the fledgling Nazi Party in Germany and in 1925 organised an antisemitic congress in Hungary. For a short time he headed the 'Race Defence Party' which espoused Nazi-style racial antisemitism. In 1935, Ferenc Szálasi (1897–1946), later to rule Hungary as Hitler's stooge, founded the party of National Will whose programme stated that 'We demand the relentless obliteration of the Jewish mentality manifested in all directions and demand the practical fostering of the inflexible Christian spirit.'

However, from 1921 to 1931 under the pragmatic, if anti-Jewish, Prime Minister Count István Bethlen (1874–1947), stability returned to Hungary and the Jews recovered from the antisemitic movement known as the White Terror. By this time the Jewish population was overwhelmingly middle and upper-middle class. Around half of all the country's industrial enterprises were owned or leased by Jews. In certain sectors, such as the chemical industry, over two-thirds of firms were owned by Jews and converts. Jews formed 37 per cent of the banking elite and were over-represented throughout the financial services. They were prominent in culture and the arts, too. No less than 73 per cent of journalists were Jewish. Yet the Jewish population had begun to shrink,perhaps a sign of anxiety about the times. Due to the loss of Galicia and Transylvania, about 40 per cent of all Hungary's Jews were now concentrated in the capital. Here the 203,000 Jews formed 20 per cent of the city's population. But the number and the proportion fell over the next decade due to emigration, conversion and slower natural growth until it stood at only 184,500. The situation of Hungarian Jewry might have remained stable had it not been for the radicalising effect of Hitler's victory in Germany and the increasing influence of the Fascist powers on countries in the Danube basin.

II

In 1931 Prime Minister Bethlen, confounded by the effects of the world-wide depression that started with the Wall Street Crash in 1929, resigned office. He was succeeded briefly by Count Károlyi whose efforts to revive the Hungarian economy were no more successful. In 1932 Horthy invited Gyula Gömbös, the strong man of the right, to form a government. Gömbös came to power with a reputation for antisemitism, but he was

prepared to do business with 'good' Jews for the benefit of the country. At the same time, as he forged closer ties with Nazi Germany and Fascist Italy, he preserved the status quo with regard to the Jews at home.

Yet the drift of policy was increasingly clear. Kálmán Darányi(1886–1939), who succeeded Gömbös as prime minister in 1936, faced demands from members of Hungary's Magyar business elite, notably the head of the National Bank, Béla Imrédy, and the military to reduce the supposed influence of the Jews in national life. The Nazi annexation of Austria in March 1938 added to this pressure. If the Hungarians were to recover any territory lost in 1919 it would only be through partnership with the new superstate of *Mitteleuropa*. In order to woo the Germans it would pay to emulate their policy towards the Jews.

So on 8 April 1938 Darányi set before parliament a bill to place a limit of 20 per cent on the proportion of Jews allowed to hold positions in the professions, commerce and business. The bill encountered vigorous opposition from Social Democrats and Liberals in the lower house but was eventually passed in May 1938. Midway through the legislative process Darányi resigned and was replaced by Imrédy who ensured its passage through the upper house even though powerful church leaders, including Jusztinián Cardinal Serédi and László Ravasz, quibbled over the definition of who it covered. Imrédy wanted to exclude Jews who had converted to Christianity after August 1919 (when the White Terror induced a wave of apostasy), while the churches wished to protect their neophytes whatever the date of conversion. After Imrédy offered some minor concessions to opponents of the bill it was passed on 29 May 1938.

The debates in parliament were notable for the poisonous and racist rhetoric directed against the Jews and Judaism. Once passed the statute officially established the existence of a 'Jewish problem' in Hungary and denigrated the Jewish presence. It legitimated the expression of even worse antisemitic views and proposals. Paradoxically its economic effect was almost negligible since there was almost no effective method of enforcement and the government was reluctant to further weaken the economy by attacking its most successful element.

Worse was to come. Hitler's success at the Munich talks in September 1938, when he achieved the break-up of Czechoslovakia and precipitated an award of territory to Hungary, confirmed Imrédy's view that the restoration of Hungarian greatness lay through ever closer ties with the Third Reich. The acquisition of Carpatho-Ruthenia, an area at the eastern extremity of Czechoslovakia that bordered north-east Hungary, which had a Jewish population of 78,000, gave him a pretext to bring in much harsher anti-Jewish legislation. This legislation, presented to the lower house of parliament on 23 December 1938, used a Nazi-style racial definition of who was a Jew. It banned Jews from public sector employment altogether and proposed to limit to 12 per cent the proportion of Jews in white-collar employment and to 6 per cent in professional bodies, journalism and the arts. It drastically curtailed the number of licenses for trade and manufacture which could be issued to Jews by municipal authorities. State and municipal bodies were mandated to limit the business they awarded to Jews.

The bill also hit at Jewish political rights. Jews were forbidden to acquire Hungarian citizenship. They were banned from standing for parliament and were denied the franchise unless they could trace their lineage back to Hungary in 1867. Jews were also banned from holding municipal office. Ominously the law also empowered the government to strip the Jews of their wealth and use it to facilitate their 'emigration'.

Once again the government faced opposition in both houses of parliament. Even reactionaries felt it was going too far and risked disrupting the economy. Churchmen in the upper house objected fervently to the racial definition of the Jews. For several weeks the two houses were deadlocked. In February 1939 Pál Teleki succeeded Imrédy (who had been forced to resign when it was shown that he had Jewish ancestry), but this only brought a more eloquent antisemite to the fore. He told parliament on 28 February, twelve days after assuming office, that 'we are engaged at present in our final struggle against Judaism'. The debate proceeded against a background of extreme anti-Jewish violence. On 2 February 1938 a right wing terror group associated with the Arrow Cross attacked the Dohány Street Synagogue with grenades, killing four Jews.

The bill was eventually passed on 4 May 1939, with a few modifications to end opposition from the upper house. Its effect on the Jewish population was immediate and debilitating. The law affected over 80 per cent of employed Jews in Budapest. Within a month 15,000 Jews had been deprived of their livelihood. A year later a further 25,000 bread-winners had been condemned to destitution.

Hungary's Jewish leadership was not passive in the face of this legislative onslaught. But its response had been ambivalent. When they saw the first anti-Jewish bill many felt that it could have been worse and advocated a policy of cooperation with the regime. This lack of confidence subverted Jewish efforts to lobby parliament and rally the democratic forces in the country. Protests by such leading artistic figures as Béla Bartók and Zoltán Kodály were of no consequence.

After the second anti-Jewish law the communal leadership realised that it could not resist alone. Envoys were sent to Jewish communities abroad, notably in Britain, to seek diplomatic intervention and financial aid. However, they weakened their case by ostentatiously refusing to have anything to do with the 'Eastern Jews' from recently annexed Carpatho-Ruthenia. In any case, by now it was too late to win foreign aid. The Jewish communities of the democracies could not even cope with the disaster that had befallen the Jews of Germany and Austria: the coffers for relief work were bare. Nazi Germany was rampant and would no longer pay heed to international bodies or foreign powers that were bent on appeasement anyway.

In May 1939 the Hungarian government was rewarded for its antisemitic policy with a handsome win in the general election. But the strategy of outflanking the far right patently failed. The Nazi-style Arrow Cross saw its representation increase from 13 to 45 deputies out of a total of 260. The Arrow Cross clamoured for ever more vicious laws against the Jews, its voice strengthened by every Nazi success. In September 1939, after signing a non-aggression pact with the Soviet Union and concluding a secret deal to carve up Poland between them, Germany invaded and defeated its eastern neighbour, Poland, in just four weeks. The following Spring, German forces conquered Denmark and Norway before turning on France and Britain. In a lightening campaign from 10 May to 22 June German forces overran Holland and Belgium, drove the British army out of continental Europe and compelled France to surrender.

In autumn 1940 Ferenc Szálasi, the Arrow Cross leader, called for legislation modelled on the Nuremberg Laws. He demanded that Jews be segregated, placed in ghettos, such as those established by the Germans in Poland, or forced labour camps, and even deported. Teleki stalled, but he committed suicide in April 1941 because he could not prevent Hungary being dragged into war with Yugoslavia, and was replaced by László Bárdossy who was pro-German. The new prime minister quickly introduced a bill for the 'protection of the racial purity of the Magyar nation'. The bill, which aped the Nuremberg Laws,

prohibited marriage between Christians and Jews, including as 'racial Jews' the children of mixed marriages and certain converts. This stipulation aroused the wrath of the churches, but only because they reserved the right to bestow or withhold marriage rights and determine who was a Christian. They did not protest on behalf of the Jews as such.

The bill, which was passed on 23 July 1941, paved the way for the complete isolation of the Jews. Subsequent anti-Jewish legislation would build on the three anti-Jewish laws of 1938–41 which the Hungarians themselves originated, formulated, debated and passed. By this time Hungarian troops were fighting side by side with the Germans in the campaign against the Soviet Union. 'Operation Barbarossa', the Nazi crusade against 'Jewish Bolshevism', marked a decisive move towards the 'Final Solution' into which Hungary was to become increasingly drawn.

III

In August 1940 Hungary, which had already got back the Upper Province (Felvidék) in November 1938 and Carpatho-Ruthenia in March 1939, was once again rewarded for its sycophancy towards Germany. As part of a massive redistribution of territory engineered by

Germany between its allies, Hungary recovered a vast tranche of Transylvania that it had lost to Romania in 1919. This transfer added 164,000 Jews to the Hungarian Jewish population bringing the total Jewish inhabitants to about 725,000, of whom around 200,000 lived in the capital. Many of the Jews in Transylvania, especially the older generation, welcomed their 'reunification' with Hungary. They were to be cruelly disappointed.

At almost the same time the government decreed that Jewish men of military age had to perform forced labour in auxiliary battalions attached to the army. In December 1940 the Hungarian army, which had already purged the Jewish officers and non-commissioned officers in its ranks, forced all Jewish servicemen into segregated units designated to perform manual labour. Conditions in the labour formations were bearable, if harsh. The first wave of conscripts was issued with khaki uniforms. They were commanded by Hungarian officers and Non-Commissioned Officers who were tough, but who rarely shared the outlook of Germans in the SS. However, once the German invasion of the Soviet Union was launched on 22 June 1941, the 50,000 men in the labour battalions assigned to the front lines were subjected to ever more hardship and danger. Yet they were protected from the massacres of Jews taking place all around them by their status in the Hungarian armed services.

Reportedly, some elements of the Hungarian Army also became involved in mass murder. In July 1941 the central office responsible for 'aliens' ordered the expulsion of foreign Jews from the North East of the country. The police and army rounded up 35,000 German, Austrian, Czech, and Slovak Jews, as well as several thousand local Jews whose citizenship was deemed 'suspicious'. In August some 18,000 of these unfortunates were deported into German-occupied Ukraine and dumped at the town of Kamenets Podolsk. Here, on 27–28 August 1941, all but about 2,000 were massacred by *Einsatzkommandos*, members of the mobile SS killing squads charged with the extermination of Communists and Jews.

Hungarian policemen and gendarmes took an active role in the deportations which were known about at the highest level. But it is not certain that the government knew about the exact fate of the deportees. When he found out in mid 1942 the Interior Minister Ferenc Keresztes-Fischer seems to have been genuinely shocked. He acted to stop any further expulsions and ordered an investigation into a massacre perpetrated by a Hungarian army unit in Újvidék (Novi

Members of the Arrow Cross in Budapest, Hungary, c. 1944.

Sad) in occupied Yugoslavia on 21–23 January 1942. On this occasion over 2,500 Serbs, including 700 Jews, were shot to death on the banks of the Danube in alleged revenge for 'partisan' actions. News of the murders sparked a public uproar and when it was proven that army headquarters and the prime minister were implicated Admiral Horthy, the head of state, felt empowered to dismiss the government. Several months later some of the alleged perpetrators were even put on trial.

The appointment of Miklós Kállay as prime minister in March 1942, following the outrage over the Újvidék massacre, seemed to offer hope to Hungarian Jews that their government would protect them from further savagery. Kállay steered a course between appeasing Nazi Germany and preserving Hungary's room for diplomatic manœuvre. The German Army had been halted before Moscow and forced to retreat along much of the Eastern Front in the winter of 1941–2. It was first major reverse suffered by the Nazi war machine and proved that it was not invincible. Kállay knew that great prudence was now required in managing Hungary's relations with the Third Reich.

Yet Kállay was a man of his time. He was from a gentry family and regarded the land as the basis of Magyar nationhood. Jewish ownership of large estates threatened this organic connection, so in June 1942 he brought in a law to enable the expropriation of Jewish-controlled estates. At this moment the German Army looked set on another victorious summer offensive against the Russians and the preamble to the bill related the bid to knock out the

Soviet Union to the attempt to curtail Jewish influence in Hungary, a coupling that would have met with approval in Berlin. The Nazis, though, would not have shared Kállay's scruples with regard to compensating Jews for assets lost as a consequence of the new law.

A few weeks later parliament passed a government bill depriving the Jewish religion of equal treatment along with other accepted denominations in Hungary. This was a further, severe financial blow to Hungarian Jewry since it deprived key institutions of state funding. No less damaging was the official degradation of the Jews and Judaism, reinforcing their pariah status.

If Kállay hoped that these anti-Jewish laws would deter his Nazi allies, or the pro-Nazi Arrow Cross, from demanding more drastic action against the Jews he was proved wrong. In September 1942 the German Foreign Office asked the Hungarian minister in Berlin, Döme Sztójay (1883–1946), to pass on a request for his government to implement the anti-Jewish measures being set in motion throughout Nazi-occupied Europe and Nazi-allied countries. These measures included the imposition of the Yellow Star, the expropriation of Jewish wealth, and deportation of Jews 'to the East'. They were all key steps towards enacting the 'Final Solution' which the Nazi leadership was working towards in the late summer or autumn of 1941. While evidence as to the exact nature and date of Hitler's order for the mass murder of all of Europe's Jewish communities remains elusive, the plans outlined by SS chief Reinhard Heydrich at a conference held in the Berlin suburb of Wannsee in January 1942 indicate that a European-wide plan for dealing with the Jews was being coordinated. The Hungarian Jews were included in Heydrich's list of Jewish communities to be destroyed, but although Jews had been deported or murdered all around Hungary, that country itself had been spared.

Kállay, with an eye on the latest dramatic developments in the war, politely rejected Germany's demands. By December 1942 the German Army was struggling to contain a massive breakthrough on the Eastern Front while a quarter of a million men were cut off in the Stalingrad pocket. The Hungarian Second Army had been all but annihilated in the Soviet offensive and the country's allegiance to Germany was strained. The government officially responded that the Jews were already subject to extensive restrictions and posed no threat to anyone. Moreover, they were serving the Hungarian war economy which was vital to the Axis military effort as a whole. Nor was there much appetite in the country for more radical impositions on the Jews who were, in any case, so numerous that such steps would be enormously difficult.

By April 1943 the Germans had stabilised the Eastern Front and the Nazi hierarchy again turned to the irksome Jewish presence in Hungary. On 17–18 April 1943 Hitler met with Horthy at Schloss Klessheim, a castle near Salzburg in Austria, to review mutual relations. Amongst other demands he made on the Hungarian Regent, the Führer insisted that Horthy approve the 'solution' of the Jewish question in Hungary. At around the same time Edmund Veesenmayer (1904–77), a high ranking member of the SS, was sent to Hungary to assess the situation. His report complained bitterly that Jews, converts and 'full Jews', held positions of authority in politics and the economy. In May, June and July the Germans again pressed the Hungarians to act. The only major concession was an agreement to supply around 3,000 men in Jewish labour battalions to work in the copper mines at Bor in Serbia. By contrast, the new Defence Minister Vilmos Nagy did his best to improve the lot of the 6,000–7,000 surviving Jewish labour servicemen in the Nazi-occupied Soviet Union.

The resistance to Nazi demands and the amelioration of the conditions in the Jewish labour companies can be seen as part of Kállay's strategy to extricate Hungary from the war. Following the German military disaster at Stalingrad in February 1943, the failure of the Kursk offensive launched by Hitler in July 1943, and the successful Allied landings in Sicily, Kállay and Horthy sent out peace feelers to the British and the Americans. When the Italian leadership deposed Mussolini on July 25 1943 and declared an armistice with the Allies on September 3, the Hungarians hoped to emulate them. Their goal was to negotiate a deal with the Western Allies to forestall either a German occupation or conquest by the Red Army, which was now rolling unstoppably towards Hungary's eastern borders.

Hitler and Himmler (head of the SS) were well aware of these moves. In December 1943 Veesenmayer made another investigative trip to Hungary and fuelled his masters' fury about Hungarian 'treachery', which he attributed to Jewish influence. When Horthy asked for the rump of the Hungarian forces on Soviet soil to be withdrawn to defensive positions on their own frontier the Germans began to think of occupying Hungary in order to abort its defection, install a puppet government, and keep its army in the field. A plan was drawn up and troops were readied.

Hitler summoned Horthy to a second meeting at Klessheim on 18 March 1944. He harangued the aged Hungarian leader and made numerous demands, but the real purpose of the parley was to keep the head of state out of the country while German units invaded and occupied key points. In accordance with 'Operation Margarethe' eleven German divisions rolled into Hungary on the morning of 19 March 1944 when Horthy was in a train heading home. On reaching the border he found Veesenmayer, an SS-*Brigadeführer*, now installed as 'Reich Plenipotentiary' and Hungary's effective ruler, responsible directly to the German Foreign Office and Hitler. The fate of Hungary's Jews was about to be sealed.

IV

At Klessheim Horthy gave his agreement that Hungary would supply Germany with some 100,000 Jewish forced labourers to construct underground factories for the manufacture of fighter aircraft. He did not mention this to his council of ministers which gathered at midday on 19 March while German tanks were still taking up positions around the capital. Rather, he debated what was best for Hungary. Ernst Kaltenbrunner (1903–46), the head of the Reich Main Security Office (the RSHA, which controlled all the police forces and the SS), visited Budapest briefly to let Horthy know that Hitler expected him to install a friendly government.

On 22 March Horthy made Döme Sztójay, the pro-German ambassador in Berlin, Prime Minister and resolved to remain as Regent in the hope of preventing the worst being done and to avoid panic amongst the Hungarian populace. But he made it clear to the new regime that the 'Jewish question' was in their hands and he wanted no part of it. Ironically, if he had conceded to the more extreme demands of the SS and appointed an Arrow Cross government it would have been a signal to the Jews that there was terrible danger ahead. But Sztójay was not tarred with that particular brush nor did his Cabinet include extreme right-wingers. On the surface it seemed that despite the German occupation not too much had changed. Indeed, such was the general calm, the Germans were able to pull out their troops before the end of the month.

Sztójay, however, was an ex-army career officer who had served as military attaché and ambassador in Berlin for many years. He knew what the Germans wanted and he was willing to give it to them. He appointed two rabid Jew-haters to positions in the Ministry of the Interior and charged them with handling Jewish affairs in cahoots with the Nazis. László Endre

(1895–1946), a highly educated, career police administrator and a personal friend of Adolf Eichmann, was made a state secretary and put in charge of administrative and legislative matters concerning the Jews. László Baky (1899–1946), an ex-army officer who had risen in the gendarmerie, was placed in control of the political aspects. Baky was a member of the Arrow Cross and a former activist in the Hungarian Nazi Party.

Between them Endre and Baky ran the 'Final Solution' in Hungary on behalf of the Nazis. They purged the civil service of opponents and replaced the regional prefects to ensure that their writ ran throughout the land. The gendarmerie, numbering about 20,000, was crucial to their plans. This force was commanded by Colonel László Ferenczy, who had German ancestry like many of those under his command. With men such as these operating as the legitimate authority, backed up by the prestige of the Regent, Admiral Horthy, the SS themselves needed to do a minimum.

This was exactly what the SS hoped for. When they prepared for their role in the occupation of Hungary the force at their disposal numbered less than 1,000 personnel. About 500–600 Gestapo men were detailed to operate under the command of Otto Winkelmann

(1894–1977), the SS Higher Police Leader for Hungary. Alongside them were 150–200 men of a *Sonderkommando*, special task force, under SS-*Obersturmbannführer* Adolf Eichmann (1906–62), head of Section IV.B.4 of the RSHA which dealt with 'Jewish affairs and emigration'.

Since March 1938, when he set up a central emigration office in Vienna, Eichmann had been perfecting the technique of 'Jewish emigration'. Until 1939 this involved asserting control over the Jewish population of conquered territory, assessing their numbers and wealth, and encouraging panic flight or expulsion where feasible. From 1940 Eichmann's office handled the forced resettlement of Jews in Poland and then throughout Europe. By mid-1941 'resettlement' entailed mass murder. The Eichmann-*Sonderkommando* included some of the most brutal and corrupt of the SS functionaries associated with the 'Final Solution': Dieter Wisliceny (1911–48) had conducted the deportation of 55,000 Slovakian Jews to Auschwitz in 1942–3 before preparing the destruction of Greek Jewry; Theodor Dannecker (1913–45) had organised the deportation of Jews from France, Bulgaria and Italy to Auschwitz in 1942–4. This diabolical *corps d'elite* set up office in the Hotel Majestic and proceeded to orchestrate the deportation and murder of the Hungarian Jews.

From the outset the Eichmann-*Sonderkommando* established its sole authority over the 'Jewish question' in Hungary. The Jewish population was left in no doubt that its fate was in their hands. One of the *Sonderkommando*'s first steps was to call a meeting with the Budapest Jewish leadership on 19 March to order the formation of a *Judenrat* or Jewish Council. This was a basic element of the strategy of genocide, tried and tested by the Nazis on the Jews in occupied countries since 1939, which was predicated on causing the least alarm amongst the potential victims and eliciting the maximum cooperation.

The *Judenrat* typically comprised of established Jewish communal leaders who were required to transmit the orders of the SS to the Jewish population. This endowed Nazi demands with a spurious air of legitimacy and eventually implicated the hapless Jews in life and death decisions. The Nazis used as leverage the desperate, but entirely normal and rational, belief amongst their victims that each demand was the last and the worst, that the nightmare would soon end, and that to refuse to cooperate was both suicidal and would certainly result in even greater disaster. By this means honourable men were placed in a impossible dilemma and

forced to become unwitting accomplices in the murder process.

In Budapest, on 21 March 1944, Samuel Stern (1874–1946), the head of the Neolog community of Pest, assumed the leading role in the Central Council of Hungarian Jews. He was aided by representatives of every strand of Jewish life. Neolog, Orthodox and Zionist Jews managed to co-operate with Stern, although this constructive attitude was rarely emulated beyond the capital. The fissures in the Hungarian Jewish population would continue to hinder the transmission of information and diminish the effectiveness of the central bodies. How much about the mass murder of the Jews outside Hungary was known by Jewish leaders in Budapest or by Jews throughout the country is still hotly debated. Refugees from Poland and Slovakia brought news of the deportations from the ghettos to the communities in which they found refuge, while escapees from Auschwitz-Birkenau sent detailed reports on the lethal preparations for the arrival of Hungarian Jews. However, ordinary Jews naturally tended to avoid the implications of what they heard and to comfort themselves with the knowledge that if they had been saved from such a fate for this long, things need not change; the alternative was unpalatable. Those at the centre continued

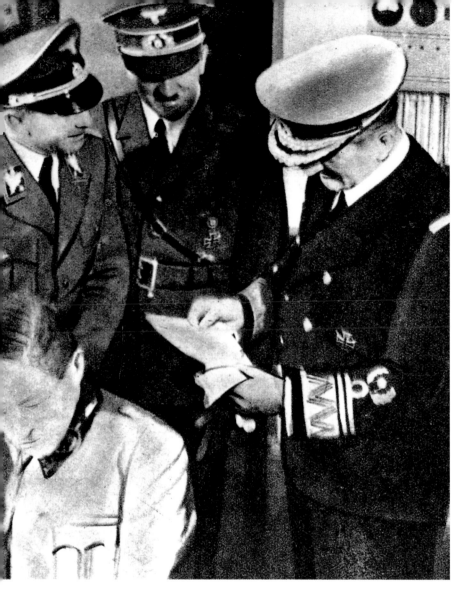

Hungarian regent Miklós Horthy
in conversation with Hitler.

been closed down. The *Journal of Hungarian Jews*, the gazette of the Council, was now the only source of information for the Jewish population. It advised Jews to stay calm, continue at work and obey the instructions of the Jewish Council. With Horthy still in office this seemed reasonable. For four years he and his ministers had protected the Jews of Hungary. They did not know of his agreement with Hitler at Klessheim or the severity of the blows struck at his own power base. Winkelmann's operatives arrested hundreds of anti-Nazi Hungarians: the possibility of resistance to Nazi demands was temporarily nullified. When it mattered, the Jews found they had few friends, and fewer left in a position to help. Over the next four weeks a hail of anti-Jewish regulations rained down on them, culminating in their ghettoisation.

Between 29 March and 28 April 1944, Jews were forced to wear the Yellow Star, banned from using personal vehicles or public transport, forbidden from using telephones or listening to the radio, and purged from any role in the public sphere such as journalism, cinema and theatre. The Nazi authorities ordered the freezing of all assets belonging to Jews held by banks and financial institutions on 20 March; four weeks later Jews were commanded to register all property and valuables.

to put their faith in the Hungarian leadership and had grounds for believing that, even if the reports were true, they would be spared.

However, ten days later Stern was called to the Hotel Majestic to hear Eichmann make his first demands: the Council had to order Jews to wear the Yellow Star, compile details of their property and wealth, designate Jewish houses and areas where Jews would be concentrated, and bring Jewish converts under its auspices.

All Jewish publications had meanwhile

Regional prefects were ordered to conduct, through the agency of the Jewish communities, a full census of the Jewish population including the compilation of lists of address. This decree was linked to the enforcement of rationing which both reassured Jews and threatened them.

Suddenly, on 16 April 1944, the first day of the Jewish festival of Pesach, Passover, Jews in Carpatho-Ruthenia were woken at dawn and ordered to assemble with a minimum of belongings prior to 'resettlement'. They were declared residents of a 'military zone' and told that they were to be evacuated for security reasons. Ghettoisation was 'legally' extended throughout the country after the promulgation of the necessary decree on 28 April. All Jews were now obliged to move to Jewish communities of over 10,000; within these large centres Jews were forced to cram into demarcated areas. The pretext was that Jews, due to their 'wealth', occupied a disproportionate amount of space and deprived Magyars of decent accommodation.

The plan for the plundering, concentration and deportation of the Jews was carefully worked out by Baky, Endre and the SS *Sonderkommando*. At a meeting on 4 April they met with key officers in the Hungarian gendarmerie and Ferenczy, whose gendarmes would do the bulk of the work. A few days later secret instructions for the conduct of concentration, ghettoisation and deporation were sent out to the prefects and mayors. Hungary was divided into six operational zones, each one corresponding to one or two gendarmerie districts.

Eichmann determined that the roundups and deportations should begin in the East and work westward, ending with the capital. He reasoned that the Eastern zones were the most threatened by the Red Army and the home to the bulk of the Orthodox Jewish population which was least liked by Christian Hungarians. The removal of the assimilated Budapest Jews would be a more ticklish matter. In fact, the onset of Allied bombing on Budapest, triggered by the German occupation, and the relentless advance of the Soviets caused the mood of the Hungarian populace to darken. The arrival of the Germans gave a massive boost to local Fascist groups and emboldened the Arrow Cross militia: antisemitic activity soared. The Gestapo and Hungarian police recorded no less than 35,000 denunciations of Jews in the first weeks of the new regime. Hungarian Christians fell upon vacated Jewish property, abandoned businesses and empty jobs like famished vultures.

The process of ghettoisation was carried out entirely by Hungarians. As Irene Zisblatt recalls, the only German presence in Polena, her home town, was two SS men on a motorcycle. The typical pattern was that on a predetermined day and hour, the mayor, police chief, gendarmes, civil servants and often local teachers would sally forth from the town hall or police station at dawn, rout out the Jews from their homes, and order them to assemble at the synagogue. The Jews were allowed to carry no more than 50 kg of baggage. From there they would be escorted to a temporary holding camp before being transported by foot or train to a ghetto or detention centre at a major urban centre with rail links to Poland. At each stage of the process teams of rapacious policemen and civilian officials evaluated and plundered their property and belongings.

In Zone I, which included Munkács, a major centre of Hasidic life and learning, and Ungvár (Užhorod in Slavic) where Renée Firestone lived, 194,000 Jews were rounded up between 16 April and 28 April. They were held in abysmal conditions for nearly a month before the deportation trains were ready. The German and Hungarian officials had not finalised the route or obtained the necessary rolling stock until a high level meeting in Vienna on 4–5 May 1944. Thereafter, however, there was no shortage of cars or locomotives: the *Wehrmacht* was eager to get its hands on Jewish forced labour and was willing to forgo the transport. From 19 to 24 May trains carried over 110,000 Jews from Munkács and similar centres via Kassa, Presov, Tarnow and Cracow to Auschwitz.

In Zone II the roundups took place from 3 May to 10 May, by which time over 98,000 Jews were behind barbed wire. They included the Jews of Kolozsvár (Cluj), a major community. In this central holding site 18,000 Jews were corralled in a brickyard with fifteen taps to supply running water. The deportation trains started to roll on 15 May; the last transport left on 8 June bringing to 290,000 the total deported.

The Jews of Zone III, which included the long-standing communities of Györ and Miskolc, were 'concentrated' between 5 and 10 June and deported between 11 and 16 June. The 53,000 Jews were taken away on twenty-three trains after horrifying scenes that aroused the protests of Bishop Apor of Györ. His entreaties to the Minister of the Interior were swept aside and he was warned that he risked imprisonment for his interference. From 16 until 26 June the Jews in Zone IV, numbering over 40,000, were swept into captivity. The treatment of the Jews of Szeged also stimulated a brave but forlorn protest by the local bishop. Nevertheless they were deported in three days between 25 and 28 June, taking the total up to 380,660 on 129 trains.

Sárvár, the home town of Alice Lok Cahana, lay in Zone V along with the historic communities of Sopron and Szombathely where Jews had lived more or less continuously for centuries. The rounding up occurred between 30 June and 3 July, with the deportations completed a mere three days later. Over 29,000 Jews, including Alice's family, were hurled towards Auschwitz. They were amongst the 410,223 sent so far. At this point the tidal wave of destruction was lapping around Zone VI, Budapest and its surroundings. Also on the days of 30 June to 3 July the Jews in the towns adjacent to the capital were herded together. On 6–8 July over 24,000 Jews, living less than a few hours travel from Budapest where nearly 200,000 Jews including Bill Basch and Tom Lantos still resided,were transported northwards. Their pitiless departure took the number of forcibly removed Jews to 434,351.

Auschwitz had been specially prepared for their arrival. In April–May a branch line was built from rail yards at Auschwitz 6km away, where prisoners had been detained for the past four years, right into the camp. The SS personnel were reinforced and,

most ominously, the number of slave workers in the *Sonderkommando* which serviced the four gas chambers and crematoria was increased from 224 to over 865. Many Greek Jews (like Dario Gabbai), who were strong and fit before they reached Birkenau, were selected for this horrific work.

By now Auschwitz-Birkenau had two purpose-built gas chambers, numbers IV and V, and two adapted from underground mortuaries, numbers II and III. Each gas chamber was connected to a bank of ovens for cremating the bodies of the victims. SS engineers and civilian experts checked the crematoria and strengthened the chimneys which would have to cope with intense and prolonged heat. Since there would still be insufficient burning capacity, nine pits were dug so that bodies could also be incinerated in the open on great pyres. Two makeshift gas chambers, converted from peasant cottages, were also brought into use to cope with the influx. Never before, or since, had such concentrated slaughter on such a scale been planned so clinically.

The process of destruction began in the brickyards and ghettos in Hungary. Marched long distances in many cases, beaten randomly on arrival, starved and denied adequate water, the Jews were weakened even before they were packed into the deportation trains. Each cattle truck or freight wagon which could accommodate 45 to 50 people was made to carry 90, 100 or more. The occupants were given one bucket for relieving themselves and one can of water. But the journey could take up to four days and by the end the conditions were abominable. Due to the heat, and it got hotter as the transportations went on into the summer, and lack of water the old, the young and the sick suffered terribly. Many died en route. Those who arrived alive were barely so, and stumbled out of the freight cars with only the thought of water in their minds. They were in no state to assess their situation or the danger they faced. The offer of a shower, clean clothes and a drink was enough to induce compliance in the throng that was marshalled on the ramp.

Only a few, like Irene Zisblatt's father, were well-enough informed or savvy enough to know that work was the only hope of survival. She lied about her age and was 'selected' for labour along with her father. The 'selection' was performed by the SS doctors, notably SS-*Untersturmführer* Josef Mengele (1911–77). He and his colleagues took advantage of the human traffic to pick twins and others for 'medical' experiments. Irene Zisblatt was fortunate in having been forced to undergo some of the least invasive or life-threatening of

these vile exercises, all of which violated medical ethics and bore no relation to genuine biological research.

An average transport from Hungary carried between 2,000 and 2,500 Jews. Of these around 10 per cent were usually chosen for labour purposes and allowed to live. The vast majority, including all the old, the young, mothers with babies or infants and the infirm, were marched or conveyed directly to the gas chambers. Sometimes they were held in nearby woods until they could be 'processed'. They were then hounded into an undressing room which appeared no different from the ante-chamber to a normal washroom. Many were compelled to send reassuring postcards to relatives at home saying they had arrived safely in 'Waldsee'. After removing their clothes the people were pushed into shower rooms; but no water appeared through the shower heads. Instead pellets of Zyklon-B, a pesticide made from hydrogen cyanide that was lethal to humans, was dropped or inserted through apertures. Within fifteen minutes everyone inside the sealed room was dead. The *Sonderkommando* team then ventilated the chamber and pulled out the corpses. Teeth with gold fillings were ripped out and bodies checked for concealed valuables. The cadavers were then hauled to the crematoria and burned. It took several hours to deal with one transport.

Those selected for work were marched to the 'central sauna', a brick building located midway between the gas chamber complexes. Here the traumatised and confused people were packed into a large hall, told to undress, their body hair was shaven, they were showered, and issued with clothing recycled from the transport. The crowds were so great that there was no time for the tattoo which usually marked those imprisoned in Auschwitz or selected to live from the transports. These 'lucky' ones were then held in the eighteen barracks in the 'quarantine camp'. The barracks were in fact prefabricated wooden sheds intended for housing cavalry horses. They had room for about 500–600 people, but were equipped for twice that number by installing crude wooden bunks that had just enough room for a person to lie on packed like a sardine in a can. The Jews lingered here for anything from a few weeks to a few months before being assigned to work parties in the neighbourhood or much further afield. Auschwitz-Birkenau had become a reservoir of slave labour meeting the insatiable demand of the German armed forces and industry for unskilled, manual workers.

Alice Lok Cahana and Renée Firestone, for instance, were sent to work in a munitions factory in October 1944.

Conditions in the 'outcamps' varied widely and depended on who ran them. Slave workers labouring on underground factories, such as the ones sent to Dora-Mittelbau, were treated appallingly and died in their thousands. Others who cleared rubble in bombed German cities or worked in factories under civilian overseers, often patrolled by home guard units composed of older men, tended to fare better.

Irene Zisblatt was sent to work inside the camp, in the 'Canada' complex. This camp within a camp was comprised of several barracks and warehouses. The cavernous storage areas were filled with the belongings of those taken from the trains: suitcases, shoes, artificial limbs, spectacles, clothes, cutlery and crockery, toiletries, precious objects, money, photographs, and much else. There were also piles of human hair. All this was sorted for distribution to German civilians or for industrial uses. An army of Jewish labourers, increased from around 1,000 to 2,000 in anticipation of the Hungarian genocide, was employed in 'Canada' to process the mountains of possessions left by the deportees. As long as the trains continued to disgorge their soiled human cargo at the ramp there was work for the *Sonderkommandos* and the *Canadakommando*. Diabolically, their survival depended on the machinery of death remaining in full employment.

Hungarian Jews are marched to the deportation centre under the watchful eyes of guards and the local population, spring 1944.

V

The Jewish leadership in Budapest followed the progress of the deportations with horror and mounting desperation. On 26 May 1944 the Jewish Council telegraphed a protest to the Minister of the Interior, Andor Jaross (1896–1946), giving details of the terrible plight of Jews interned in Northern Transylvania. They pleaded to be allowed to send aid to the camps and ghettos. A week later they addressed a letter to Eichmann echoing these points. Needless to say they were ignored. On 7 June the Council submitted a memorandum to Prime Minister Sztójay giving more damning information on the fate of their brethren. Persisting in the belief that there was some rationality about what was happening they suggested that it would be of more benefit to Hungary if the Jews were kept in the country even if it was necessary to hold them in camps.

These protestations appeared feeble in the face of such a crisis. In mid June labour servicemen upbraided the Council leaders in their office. But what else could they do? On 16 June the authorities ordered the Budapest Jews from their homes into specially designated Yellow Star houses, the first stage of concentration prior to deportation from the capital itself. This measure sent a wave of terror through the Jews, but in the short term the Council had just a week to move thousands of people and set up facilities for them ranging from schools to soup kitchens. It was difficult enough coping with this without taking on board the catastrophe occurring hundreds of miles away. Only the Orthodox leader Fülöp Freudiger seemed alert to the fate of

'Eastern Jews' and plucked scholars and rabbis from over half a dozen doomed communities.

In any case the Council's options were almost non-existent. Their efforts to reach Horthy to plead for his intercession were stymied because their old contacts amongst the liberal-minded nobility had been arrested or gone to ground. Even rich and ennnobled Jews, such as the families of Ferenc Chorin and Baron Jenö Weiss, who controlled the Manfréd Weiss industrial conglomerate, were bargaining for their lives and were glad to escape from Hungary with just a fraction of their wealth.

Even if they had got through to the Regent it would have done no good: he already knew what was happening and let it be so. There were no other centres of resistance: barely a voice was raised by Hungarian gentiles against the ghettoisation or deportations. The Budapest Jewish leadership thought only in terms of getting relief to communities in the provinces and had no notion of sponsoring resistance. They were Hungarian citizens and they believed their security lay in continuing to act as law-abiding members of the nation. Each Jew had to stand on his or her own rights: to conceive of collective civil disobedience contradicted the time-honoured ethos of Hungarian Jewry.

Nor was this such a foolish perspective as it seemed in hindsight. Successive Hungarian governments had shielded them from anti-Jewish violence and deportations. Rather than acting as a tocsin, knowledge of the atrocities befalling the Jews of Slovakia, Poland and Russia in 1941–3 had the opposite effect: their exclusion from the catastrophe of European Jewry actually butressed their conviction that Hungary was different and that they were safe. As it became clear that the tide of war was running against Germany there seemed even less reason for anxiety: the most sensible thing to do was to sit tight and trust the government. Without a revolution in thinking they could not have acted otherwise.

Even the small Zionist movement, which did think in activist terms and considered the Jews a national minority, did not differ that much in practice. In January 1943 a Relief and Rescue Committee was set up in Budapest to assist Polish and Slovakian Jews escaping the death camps by illegally crossing into Hungary. These refugees brought news of the genocide to the North, but this did not seem to apply to the Hungarians. On the contrary, they were in the fortunate position of being able to assist about 15,000–20,000 refugees who found shelter in Hungary.

The leading figures in the Relief and Rescue Committee were Ottó Komoly (1892–1944), president of the Hungarian Zionist Association, Dr Rezsö Kasztner (1906–57), a former journalist and communal worker, and Joel Brand (1907–64), a businessman. In December 1943 they began to consider more radical measures. At the urging of members of the underground Zionist youth movements in Poland who had reached Hungary, and egged on by Zionist representatives in Turkey who had a panoramic view of the Jewish debacle, they embarked on steps for physical resistance. However, due to the repeated call up of Jewish men for labour service there were few young, able-bodied Jewish males left in Hungary. The burden of resistance fell on those under 17 or over 40 years old. Nevertheless, in the New Year they set about constructing 'bunkers': hideouts in basements and cellars. They also tried to acquire arms. This was so slow and difficult to achieve that those with an appetite for combat usually tried to reach the partisans in Yugoslavia; few made it alive. These incipient preparations were overwhelmed by the speed of the German occupation and what ensued.

After 19 March 1944 the Zionists followed three strategies. Some youngsters were sent on missions to warn provincial Jewry of the impending danger. In the areas bordering Romania groups were assembled to trek to safety across the border, known as *tiyul*. Sadly many Orthodox Jewish communities, which were anti-Zionist, refused to heed the warnings issued by irreligious young men from the capital bearing only vague credentials. However, they did arrange for some 2,000 Jews to reach Romania alongside 5,000–6,000 who made their way singly or in groups on their own initiative.

Back in Budapest the Zionist underground redoubled its efforts to create hiding places and also set about forging false papers to enable Jews to go underground. Finally, Komoly and Kasztner embarked on negotiations with the Hungarian and German powers. The latter proved to be the most promising and ultimately most controversial efforts at rescue.

Kasztner and Komoly had previously been in contact with the Jewish Council of Slovakia, based in Bratislava, which had prior experience of such dealings. In 1942 its leaders had paid a large bribe to Wisliceny which they believed, wrongly as it turned out, had persuaded him to call a halt to further deportations of Jews from Slovakia. The following year they negotiated with Wisliceny again in the hope that they could bribe the SS to abort the mass murder programme as a whole.

The Hungarian Zionists knew about these moves, so when Wisliceny arrived in Budapest they anticipated that with enough cash they could buy safety for their people. Wisliceny, a man of almost bottomless corruption and cynicism, was only too happy to string them along.

Kasztner and Komoly revived the proposal first made to Wisliceny in Bratislava for a $2 million bribe to win termination of the deportations. He responded favourably and suggested that a down payment of $200,000 in Hungarian currency would be a suitable token of good faith. In fact, Wisliceny had absolutely no authority or power to make such promises. While Kasztner and Komoly, with the agreement of Samuel Stern, scrambled to find the cash he left town in pursuit of his orders to supervise the ghettoisation and transporation of the Jews in the East of the country. When his Jewish contacts expressed a sense of betrayal he coolly offered to save 600 Jews of their choosing. Such a gesture was also calculated to nurture the belief that they could save lives and keep them occupied trying to secure salvation by negotiation rather than engaging in forms of resistance that would seriously inconvenience the SS.

Soon afterwards Eichmann himself took up the negotiations. On 25 April 1944 Kasztner raised the stakes by offering a new deal: if the SS would stop the deportations the Jews would secure food and war material for the Germans. Eichman was intrigued by the possibilities this offered and passed it on to SS-*Standartenführer* Kurt Becher who was acting on behalf of the SS economic organisation. Becher, in turn, relayed the message to Himmler, head of the SS and deputy to the Führer himself. Himmler hated Jews as much as Hitler, but he was willing to trade a few Jewish lives for economic, military or diplomatic advantage. He had no desire or intention to actually halt the genocide permanently or temporarily. Indeed, this would have been unthinkable without Hitler's express permission; but he authorised Eichmann to proceed with the negotiations to see where they would lead. In the Nazi world view the Jews were all-powerful: Churchill and Roosevelt were just their puppets. Maybe the offer to save a few Jews would decisively affect the course of the war.

Around 15 May, just when the deportations began, Eichmann informed Kasztner and Brand that he approved of their idea and wanted them to put it to World Jewry and the Allies. The deportations would be halted and the Jews would be allowed to emigrate (to anywhere except Palestine) in return for tons of coffee, tea, soap, tungsten and 10,000 trucks for use on the Eastern Front.

Eichmann ordered Brand to transmit the offer, but he insisted that he be accompanied by Bandi Grosz, a disreputable character who was tangled up with the intelligence operations of Germany, Hungary and America.

The involvement of Grosz doomed the mission although Brand and Kasztner did not realise this for some time. Himmler's agents had tasked Grosz to sound out the Western Allies (Britain and the USA) on the prospects of a separate peace, allowing Germany to concentrate its forces against the Red Army. The British and the Americans, who were anxious that Stalin be kept within the anti-German alliance and understood the nature of the ploy, deftly avoided the bait set by Himmler.

Brand reached Istanbul on 19 May and described the 'trucks for blood' offer to incredulous representatives of the Jewish Agency, the quasi-government of the Palestinian Jews. The British High Commissioner for Palestine, Sir Harold MacMichael, was less than thrilled when he got wind of the offer. On the one hand he suspected a trap set for the Allies; on the other, if the offer was genuine, he didn't want thousands of Jews heading for Palestine and upsetting the Arabs. On 31 May 1944 the British War Cabinet debated the proposal and decided it was a deadly ruse. Zionist leaders in Palestine and

London, including Chaim Weizmann, begged the British not to drop the deal completely and to at least drag out the negotiations, but without any success. Brand was imprisoned by the British in Aleppo as he made his way to see the Zionist leadership in Jerusalem, and was prevented from returning to Budapest. On 19 July 1944 the story was broken to the world's press and the scheme was wrecked.

Brand also took to the West a plea to bomb the railroads leading to Auschwitz. The idea of interdicting the transports or even bombing the death camp was first put to the Allies by Slovakian Jewish leaders in May 1944. It was echoed by the Jewish Agency in Jerusalem and Weizmann in London in late June 1944. Controversy has since raged over the British and American response to these desperate urgings. Winston Churchill famously minuted to Anthony Eden, the Foreign Secretary, to put the matter to the Royal Air Force Bomber Command 'get everything you can out of them'. But on 3 August 1944 Bomber Command replied that there was insufficient intelligence data to direct long-range bombers to the target.

John Pehle of the War Refugee Board, charged with the succour of persecuted Jews, transmitted a similar plea to John J.

McCloy, the Assistant Secretary of War. Finally, after many such entreaties, McCloy summed up the attitude of the War Department in a definitive letter to Leon Kubowitzki, head of the Rescue Department of the World Jewish Congress, on 14 August 1944: 'Such an operation could only be executed by the diversion of considerable air support essential to the success of our forces now engaged in decisive operations elsewhere and would in any case be of such doubtful efficacy that it would not warrant the use of our resources.' Yet the US American Army Air Force was already flying missions against the synthetic rubber plant at Monowitz, six miles from Birkenau.

Sufficient intelligence would have been available if the relevant personnel had been advised of the data brought out by two Jewish prisoners, Rudolf Vrba and Alfred Wetzler, who escaped from Birkenau on 7 April 1944. They reached the Jewish community of Slovakia two weeks later and warned the Slovak Jewish leadership that Auschwitz was being prepared for a massive new intake of Jews. Their report, known as the 'Auschwitz Protocols', was sent via intermediaries to the Vatican and Switzerland where Jewish activists brought it to the attention of Allied diplomats. With the help of the report it would have been possible to brief experts to derive the essential data from the aerial photographs taken by reconnaissance planes preparing for the raids on Monowitz. When these photographs were made public in 1978 they created a public stir and raised anew the question of why Auschwitz-Birkenau was not bombed.

Bombing the railroads would have been the least effective measure since tracks were easily repaired, but a raid on Birkenau, even if it had caused casualties amongst the Jews (many of whom were anyway prepared to die in an attempt to blow up the gas chambers, as the revolt by the *Sonderkommando* in October 1944 showed) might have slowed down the killing process significantly. A successful raid in early July could have saved tens of thousands of lives.

Kasztner managed to get 388 Jews out of his native Kolozsvár on 10 June and later negotiated with Eichmann for a train load of Jews to be kept 'on ice' to show serious intent. After an unseemly scramble that involved the exchange of large sums of money 1,684 Jews were saved in this way; most of these were prominent Jews had been chosen through the agency of the Jewish Council to represent the spectrum of Jewish political and religious life in Hungary. A lot were related to activists on the Relief and Rescue Committee, a fact which subsequently led to charges of corruption. The fortunate Jews were held in a special section of Bergen-Belsen concentration camp until they were sent to Switzerland in two groups in August and December 1944. Their liberation was the culmination of complex negotiations involving Kasztner, Kurt Becher and Saly Mayer, a Swiss Jew who acted for the Joint Distribution Committee. Kasztner was also able to prod Eichmann into sending around 20,000 Jews to Strasshof concentration camp in Austria, rather than Auschwitz, where three-quarters survived the war.

VI

The news of the deportations and detailed information about Auschwitz-Birkenau which reached the Free World in mid June finally stirred international opinion. The Vrba-Wetzler report was given to the local representative of the Vatican who passed it on to Rome. On 20 June 1944 a papal envoy arrived to interrogate the men personally. He was convinced by what he heard and five days later Pope Pius XII sent a telegram to Horthy appealing to 'the Hungarian government once again not to continue its war against the Jews' and 'to save many unfortunate people from suffering and pain'.

The President of the United States of America, Franklin Delano Roosevelt, issued a statement on 24 March 1944. He called the systematic slaughter of the Jews by the Nazis 'one of the blackest crimes of all history' warned that 'hundreds of thousands of Jews who, while living under persecution, have at least found a haven from death in Hungary and the Balkans, are now threatened with annihilation' and declared that 'none who participate in these acts of savagery shall go unpunished'. This had as little effect as subsequent declarations by the Senate Foreign Relations Committee and the House Foreign Affairs Committee. On 26 June, however, Roosevelt sent a personal message to Horthy demanding an end to the deportations and again threatening retribution. King Gustav of Sweden added his voice to the protests two days later.

These pleas compounded Horthy's sense of unease. Earlier in June he told the Swiss military attaché that he was worried that the persecution of the Jews was having an adverse effect on Hungary's image and damaging the possibility of developing contacts with the Western Allies. By now he was sure Germany had lost the war: the Allied invasion of France had evidently succeeded. In the East the Red Army rolled forward inexorably. When American bombers raided Budapest on 2 July 1944 Horthy feared that the long arm of retribution was already knocking at his door.

Horthy's change of heart was just in time to save the estimated 164,000 Jews in Budapest, the sole remnant of Hungarian Jewry. In five chaotic days between 16 and 21 June the Jews had been forced to move into about 1,800 designated 'Yellow Star Houses'. The Eichmann-*Sonderkommando* and the head of the gendarmerie had fixed the 10 July for the date of the deportations from the capital.

During a series of meetings of the Council of Ministers in mid June the opponents of the deportations mustered the strength to raise objections.On 23 June 1944 Horthy summoned Endre and Baky to account for the atrocities he had heard about from his own son as well as trusted friends such as Count Bethlen. To Horthy's annoyance they lied blatantly. At the end of the month he forced the Minister of the Interior to relieve Endre and Baky of their responsibility for Jewish affairs. Baky now took matters into his own hands and conspired with the Germans and the gendarmerie to oust Horthy and bring about the final deportations. Horthy preempted the coup by bringing loyal army units into the capital and ordering the gendarmes to leave. He then told Veesenmayer that the deportations had to stop and required the removal of the

Gestapo. On 7 July 1944 Horthy publicly announced an end to the deportations. However, the deportations continued for two more days, liquidating the Jews in the cities surrounding Budapest.

For a few weeks it seemed as if the trauma of the Hungarian Jews was over. In successive announcements Horthy declared that the government would recognise the passports issued to 500 Jews by the Swedes and would permit the departure of about 7,000 Jews with certificates to emigrate to Palestine. On 7 August he sacked Jaross and on 25 August finally removed Sztójay. The new prime minister, General Géza Lakatos, was a Horthy loyalist whose chief objective was to disengage Hungary from its Nazi ally and make peace with the Allies in order to forestall a Soviet occupation. As part of his diplomatic offensive he ordered the restrictions on Jews to be relaxed and wrested control of Jewish matters from the SS.

On 8 October 1944 Hungary formally sought peace terms with the Allies. Horthy knew this would provoke Hitler's wrath so he prepared the army to resist a second German intervention and planned the arrest of pro-Nazi Arrow Cross leaders. But Hitler had anticipated such moves. The SS sheltered the Arrow Cross cadres while SS-Standartenführer Otto Skorzeny and his elite unit went into action, kidnapping Horthy's son and disabling the resistance. Horthy's coup totally misfired. Instead, the Nazis put Ferenc Szálasi and the Arrow Cross into power at last. Horthy was forced to sign over authority to Szálasi before being spirited away to captivity in Bavaria. The agony of the surviving Hungarian Jews was to be prolonged by four more ghastly months.

VII

The Arrow Cross Party and militia, also known as the Nyilas, celebrated their assumption of power with a five-day reign of terror that claimed the lives of hundreds of Jews. Eichmann quickly returned to Budapest to complete his unfinished business with the zealous help of the new Minister of the Interior Gábor Vajna, a fanatical Nazi with a diminishing grasp of reality. Even as the Red Army was battering at the suburbs of Budapest, Vajna was ordering that streets named after Jews should receive new nomenclature. But the 150,000–160,00 Jews in the capital and the 150,000 in forced labour units faced a far more serious threat.

On 20 October 1944 all Jews aged 16 to 60 were ordered to report for labour service. Each day for a week batches of men and women were taken from the 'Yellow Star Houses' until 35,000 had been removed to camps on the outskirts of Budapest. Meanwhile around 50,000 labour servicemen were sent to Germany at Eichmann's request. On 8 November about 25,000 Jews were ordered to march towards Austria. Thousands out of the more than 70,000 Jews sent on these death marches in the late autumn of 1944–5 perished or were shot in miserable conditions at countless barely remembered spots by roadsides, in barns, or makeshift camps. Those who survived ended up in the no-less perilous confines of Mauthausen and Gunskirchen concentration camps.

Those remaining in Budapest were turfed out of their homes and forced into a walled ghetto in the heart of the Jewish district between 29 November and 3 December 1944. By January of the following year 70,000 Jews were crammed into 0.3 km sq. There was no space to even bury the dead so that 3,000 corpses piled up alongside garbage and homeless refugees. A ghetto council created by the Arrow Cross regime struggled to maintain order and food supplies, but the Jews had to subsist on half of what was required to sustain life. As the Red Army surrounded the capital the Arrow Cross militiamen directed their rage against the Jews, launching murderous excursions into the ghetto and Jewish houses or forcing groups of Jews down to the Danube where they were tormented and shot in large batches. About 17,000 Jews were slaughtered amidst this mayhem including several members of the Jewish Council. One of the last casualties was Ottó Komoly, who was dragged out of the Ritz Hotel to the Arrow Cross headquarters and murdered.

During these blood crazed months the representatives of the neutral powers saved thousands of lives. Until then the international response to the occupation of Hungary had been slow and fitful. In March 1944 the Swedish minister in Budapest, Carl Ivan Danielsson, had warned his government of the impending cataclysm and sought instructions. The Swedish Cabinet replied that 'You may in exceptional cases according to your judgment issue provisional passports' valid for six months to Jews with close family or business ties to Sweden. Danielsson was careful with his remit even though the Swedish legation was besieged with supplicants. By the end of June some 650 Jews with genuine Swedish connections had been given Swedish diplomatic papers. Gösta Engzell, the head of the foreign passport division of the Swedish government's legal department interpreted the rules as generously as possible and aided Per Anger, the Chargé d'Affairs in Budapest, to help even unlikely cases. But

it was not until the arrival of Raoul Wallenberg that the number of protective documents rose significantly.

Raoul Wallenberg (1912–47?) was a scion of the wealthy and powerful banking dynasty that controlled a large segment of the Swedish economy. His uncles, Jacob and Marcus, ran the Enskilda Bank and various industries that were closely bound up with the Nazi war economy, a family connection that cast a long shadow. Thanks to his business links in Central Europe and contacts with Swedish Jews his name was put forward as an agent of the War Refugee Board (WRB) to work in Budapest. The WRB had been created by order of Roosevelt in January 1944 with the express task of saving Jews where possible. Unfortunately, at least one of those involved with the WRB's work in Sweden who liaised with Wallenberg in setting up his mission also worked for American intelligence. This association and his family ties probably led to his detention by Soviet forces in January 1945. Many suspect that Wallenberg was murdered while in Soviet captivity, probably around 1947. It was a tragic fate for a man who galvanised the rescue effort in Budapest, even though he arrived too late to have any effect on the deportations from the rest of the country.

Just three days after his arrival

Wallenberg cajoled Sztójay into accepting the issuance of 5,000 Swedish diplomatic passes to Jews intending to go to Palestine. Since the Jewish resistance set up an underground printing press to forge copies of these passes the effect of Wallenberg's initiative was multiplied many times over. Bill Basch was one of the Jewish underground engaged in this illicit rescue work until he was caught while distributing passes and sent to Buchenwald concentration camp.

After the Szálasi coup Wallenberg went in person to the detention camps around Budapest and the railheads used for deportations to demand the exemption of Jews who had Swedish protection. Bill Basch was one of those who owed his live to Wallenberg. Wallenberg also persuaded the Arrow Cross regime to permit the establishment of an 'international ghetto' where all those with papers from neutral powers could be gathered together for greater safety from marauding Fascist gangs. For a short while over 15,000 Jews were protected in this way. In addition the Swedish legation bought houses for Jews to live in or for use as hospitals and orphanages and confirmed on them an extra-territorial status.

Wallenberg worked closely with the diplomats of other non-belligerent countries. In April 1944 Charles Lutz, the Swiss Consul, arranged with his government to guarantee 7,000 Jews who had emigration certificates to go to Palestine. Lutz enhanced the effect of these passes by interpreting them as securing the entire family of the named person. He also acquired a number of buildings where Jews could stay under Swiss diplomatic protection. Switzerland meanwhile attempted to broker a deal with the British whereby would-be emigrants would be allowed to leave for Palestine; it foundered on British reluctance to admit Jews to the 'Jewish National Home'.

Under the Szálasi regime Swiss officials continued to distribute diplomatic papers using young Jews from the Zionist youth movements as couriers. Tom Lantos, who escaped from a labour camp where he had been sent for refusing to wear the Yellow Star, returned to Budapest to become one of these audacious couriers. He stayed in a Swedish-protected house when he was not braving Arrow Cross patrols in the city streets.

Thanks to a few courageous delegates the International Committee of the Red Cross (ICRC), based in Switzerland, finally broke free of its bureaucratic and myopic stance towards the Jews. Jean de Bavier, the delegate in Hungary from October 1943 to May 1944, took a keen interest in the Jews and prodded his superiors to take some action to help them. He warned the Geneva headquarters of the ICRC that the German occupation boded ill and requested instructions to protect the Jews. This forthright communication seems to have provoked his recall: Max Haber, the head of the ICRC, reiterated that it was no business of the Red Cross to interfere in local civilian matters and would jeopardise their international work to do so. Friedrich Born, who replaced de Bavier, followed in his predecessor's conscientious footsteps and transmitted to Geneva unvarnished accounts of the anti-Jewish measures in May–June1944. But it was not until the 'Auschwitz Protocols' reached Geneva that he was permitted any leeway. On 5 July 1944 Born finally saw Horthy to object against the deportations.

In late July 1944 an ICRC delegation visited the internment camps at Kistarcsa and Sárvár but Born was too late to prevent the deportation of 2,700 Jews by Eichmann in defiance of Horthy's orders to stop the transports. Beginning in August the ICRC began to take over houses in Budapest, affixing to them a sign that warned intruders against interfering with a neutral authority. Born orchestrated a meeting of representatives of the Neutrals on 17 October, soon after the Szálasi takeover. The meeting brought together Swedish, Swiss, Spanish, Portuguese and

Vatican delegates who agreed to concert their efforts to provide safe houses for Jews, passes and other forms of support such as soup kitchens. The ICRC issued about 15,000 protective passes and made it possible for Dr Gábor Sztehló to set up an orphanage that provided refuge for 5,000–6,000 Jewish children.

The Vatican, which had played an important role in procuring the 'halt' order in July 1944, continued to play a laudable, if belated, humanitarian role. The Papal Nuncio, Monsignor Angelo Rotta, repeatedly interceded with Sztójáy and Szálasi on behalf of converts and occasionally for 'full Jews'. The Nuncio cooperated with the other Neutrals, recognised the diplomatic documents they issued to Jews, and arranged for several thousand to dwell safely in houses that were designated as Vatican territory. By the end of 1944 some 2,500 Jews officially, and perhaps as many as 15,000 unofficially, held Vatican papers.

On 17–18 January 1945 soldiers of the Red Army broke through the defenses of Budapest and liberated Pest, the area where the ghetto was located and the uncertain domicile of almost all the surviving Jews. The entire city was liberated weeks later. The Soviets found about 70,000 Jews in the ghetto and 50,000 either in hiding or living under foreign protection. Liberation

*The hanging of Ferenc Szálasi,
former head of the Arrow Cross.
Found guilty by a People's Tribunal
of war crimes, he was executed on
12 March 1946.*

took even longer for the labour servicemen and deportees in Germany or other areas under German control. Irene Zisblatt waited until the camp she was in was liberated by American troops during the last weeks of the war. Alice Lok Cahana was rescued from the hellish precincts of Bergen-Belsen, along with many thousands of Hungarians who had been transferred there from Birkenau and other camps, when the Germans surrendered the camp to British forces on 15–16 April. Bill Basch clung to life in Dachau until it was overrun by American troops on 29 April. Renée Firestone was finally released from her torment by Russian troops on the very last day of the war in Europe, 8 May 1945.

In addition to the 120,000 Jews found alive in Budapest, when the war was over about 25,000 men and women trickled back to their homes in the capital from labour units and concentration camps. Some 46,000 returned to the provinces and about 65,000 survivors made their way back to areas now recovered by Czechoslovakia, Romania, and Yugoslavia. Only 100,000 Jews, like those interviewed here, had survived forced labour, the deportations, death marches and the concentration camps.

Transfer of Jews to the ghetto in Körmend, Hungary. Spring 1944

A crowd of Jews, distinguishable by their yellow stars, are rounded up by German soldiers in Budapest. Immediately after the overthrow of the Horthy government by the Arrow Cross on 15 October 1944, the new Szálasi regime terrorised Jews living in and around Budapest. The Arrow Cross also began broadcasting antisemitic propaganda to incite the non-Jewish population against the 'Jewish-Bolshevik menace'. Rumours circulated then that a group of Jewish labour servicemen had offered armed resistance to the Arrow Cross and so the regime ordered all Yellow Star houses to be sealed off for ten days. Thousands of Jews were then rounded up and marched to collection points; their immediate fate remained uncertain. However, after vigorous protests by representatives of neutral governments and ordinary Hungarians, the regime backed down and allowed the Jews to disperse back to their homes.

*An Arrow Cross soldier detaining a
Jewish man in Budapest, 1944.*

Jews rounded up by the SS and Arrow Cross personnel are beaten while being herded into the City Theatre on Kálmán Tisza Square, Budapest. October 1944.

Men and women are marched through the streets of Budapest to deportation trains during the Arrow Cross regime (c. October–November 1944).

ALICE LOK CAHANA

We lived in a town called Sárvár, in Hungary, close to the Austrian border. It was a small town. Since the tenth century Jewish people lived in this town. There were three synagogues – the Orthodox, the Reform, and a small synagogue called BetHaMidrash. Not far from our house was the market, where every morning the peasants from the countryside would bring fresh food in baskets, and Mother would go and buy wonderful peaches, cherries and grapes for our family and for Grandfather, who lived with us.

Grandfather was beloved by the community. For many years he was the president of the Jewish community, and he was a very charitable man. I remember when I was maybe ten years old, walking with him in the park, next to the castle where he admired the beautiful spring flowers, when a teenage boy hurled a rock at him that barely missed his head. When I wanted to throw a rock back at the boy in anger, Grandfather stopped me, saying, 'We don't do this.' Soon after that I understood that the street was not safe for us Jews. Only on Sabbath were we permitted to play in the park.

Sabbath was always beautifully celebrated in our house. After breakfast we would help to clear the table and make the room presentable, because the elders of the community would come to our house and study Torah. Grandfather was a wonderful leader who also took care of the poor children in town. If somebody was an orphan, before their wedding he would take care that that person got everything that was needed for the wedding and for their trousseau.

There were four children in our family. Edith was the eldest. She already helped in the office of my family's carpet-weaving factory. I looked up to her so much,

Alice Lok Cahana's family in 1942. (From left to right) Cousin Ernsti Glück, Alice Lok, Mother Tereza (Teri) Lok, Father Jenö Lok, Grandfather Adolf Schwarz, Edith Lok, Öcsi Lok.

Alice's sister, Edith Lok

Alice's father, Jenö Lok

Monday mornings and coming back Thursday night. We would go to the railroad station to pick him up and he always had some goodies for us. It was always wonderful when Father came home on Thursday nights, and we were sad when he had to leave on Mondays.

Mother took care of Grandfather, but she wanted all of us to live in Budapest and not have Father going back and forth. Father always promised that we would move to Budapest, but then Grandmother died and Mother had to take care of Grandfather: she had to postpone moving. So it never happened.

because she was already what I wanted to be: seventeen years old and independent. She would go at night, when nobody could see her, to take food – some flour and sugar from the pantry – to the poor people. I thought this was such a beautiful act; to give something away because we had a little more than others. So Edith was always special.

I had two little brothers, one was ten and one was five. I took care of the five-year-old – I'd always felt as if I was the mother – and gave him love and attention and dressed him nicely. His name was Imi. My other brother's name was Öcsi. Father was a very handsome man. He had an office in Budapest and commuted, leaving on

or dinner, whatever they needed. Some Jewish people, who had run away from Poland, came and told stories. Stories that Jews were gathered and taken away from their homes. And I remember we didn't believe them. It couldn't happen, not in the twentieth century, we said. It was inconceivable. I, as a child, loved my town, and Grandfather was always optimistic. 'Nothing can happen to us,' he said. We had been in this town from the beginning of time. We were part of this town. Judaism was our religion, but we were Hungarians by nationality. We were hard-working, contributing,

Alice's mother, Tereza (Teri) Schwarz Lok

(Counterclockwise from upper right) Alice's Uncle Salamon (Zalme) Schwarz, Aunt Terus and cousins Robert and Andor. All pictured on these two pages were killed in the Holocaust.

The first time I really felt antisemitism was when I went to the factory one day and saw a swastika. I talked to one of our workers: 'How can you put a swastika in the workers' dining room?' They said, 'Oh, don't you know they'll take you away from here and make soap out of you.' I replied, 'You know, if you wash yourself in good-smelling soap, remember it's me.' Answering him back, I at least didn't feel like he'd clobbered me. But I never could figure out why we were hated. I always asked myself, 'Why am I different? What am I doing that's so wrong?'

Because Grandfather was the head of the community, the Rabbi always sent over strangers, and they would get lunch

Locals watch occupation forces entering their town in Hungary, spring 1944.

tax-paying. Our factory supported a lot of people.

On 19 March 1944, the Germans, the SS, entered our town. They circled it several times, so it looked like it was a big army, but actually it was just a small group of tanks. But that day, it became real. Very threatening. Right away there was a decree that we could not leave our houses in the evenings and, soon after that, they said they would take us to a ghetto. We had never heard the word 'ghetto', but it meant we would leave our house.

I watched my mother's face. How was she reacting? Was she panicking? Scared? What amazed me was that she went to the market and bought flowers. She bought violets. She came home with the flowers and quietly arranged them in a vase. I

thought, then maybe it's not so terrible. Maybe all these frightening things will not come to a horrible end. In retrospect, I see this was how she tried to strengthen us. I admire her so much, because this little gesture gave us hope.

Shortly after came a decree that we would have to leave our house. We had to pack up twenty-five kilos of baggage to take with us. At first we didn't understand – what do you take? Think about your home, your own home, what would you take that is twenty-five kilos? How much is twenty-five kilos? Do you take the pillows, do you take your dishes, what do you take? What is precious? What is necessary? We had to sort all this out in a couple of hours.

Our factory was given over to two non-Jewish men, Mr Kroger and Mr Oswald. Mr

Kroger occupied our house with his wife. Jews could not own a factory, said one of the decrees. Jews cannot be landlords. They cannot own a home. When we left home, we were all carrying bags. The pillows and the blankets were tied in a bundle, which we children carried. I was so ashamed.

They took us not far from our house, maybe because Grandfather was respected. The Rabbi, Grandfather and about ten or twelve families were taken to the street where the Jewish school and synagogue were. And so we were in this schoolroom, with our pillows and some mattresses and a couple of pots. And a makeshift table and we could cook on a burner. No hot water. Our whole household was suddenly reduced to one room, and that served for sleeping, cooking and eating.

The ghetto was watched on both sides; they erected a little gate and by the gate there was a gatehouse, and a *zsandár*, a Hungarian policeman, stood on both sides. The able men who could work were sent to a work camp.

Jews are marched down a main street in Köszeg, Hungary for deportation, May 1944.

'Edith, you know, they took us to the wrong place. They will come soon and apologise. This is an insane asylum. Someone will apologise.'

A couple of days later, Father took a chance. In the middle of the night he decided to go to Budapest, where his office was, which was six hours away by train. There was a decree that Jews were not allowed to travel on the regular railroad, and the *zsandár* was at the station, stopping people and checking their papers. But Father was so elegant, he just lifted his hat, greeted the Germans in German, and passed by. Nobody stopped him, and so he went to Budapest.

The rest of us stayed in our small ghetto for a few weeks before being moved to join the others in the sugar factory. A couple of days later we were taken with all the other Jews to the train station, where we were put into cattle cars.

While we were walking through the town to the train station, I remember thinking it was like when the Jews went out of Egypt. We were walking past our house in a big group of people. At first I didn't want to look at our house, and then I looked. And there were Mr and Mrs Kroger by the window, looking at us. I felt so ashamed, so humiliated. How could they watch us going by? But they just watched. And then the gate of our house opened and our dog ran out. I prayed he would not recognise us; let him not run after us, because the SS guard who was taking us to the train station probably would have shot him. And that was the last I saw of our home.

The only word heard is 'rush'. Rush, rush, rush'. Don't think, just get up fast. People are coming after you. I was pushed into a cattle car while holding my little brother's hand, and we were pushed into the corner. It is horrendous, all these people all mashed together, mashed like sardines. And it was very, very hot. There was a bucket in the middle and they said it was for sanitary use, and then another bucket for drinking water. They closed the doors. In our cattle car was our neighbour, Mrs Eckstein, who was nine months pregnant, and I prayed, 'Please don't let her give birth in this horrible place.' And I glanced at Grandfather – distinguished community leader – sitting on a heap of luggage in the suffocating heat. I had brought a book with me, Stephan Zweig's *The Restless Heart*, thinking I would read on the train, not imagining they would put us in cattle cars like animals. Instead I just wanted to shut it all out, stand in a corner and try to get a little air. Talk about fear. It is beyond fear. As the bucket filled up, the odour became unbearable.

I kept asking Edith, 'Where are they taking us, where are they taking us?' Nobody answered, nobody knew. People did not talk so as not to frighten the children; they did not talk because it was

so hot their mouths were dry; they did not talk because there was nothing to say.

Five days later we arrived. The first thing everybody asked when the train stopped was, 'Where are we? Where are we? What's the name?' Looking out through the cracks I could make out some letters. It was a very strange name: Auschwitz. Half dead, hot, I tried to look for Grandfather and I couldn't find him in the dark. Then they opened the door and suddenly the light hit us. Because our eyes had been used to this darkness for four or five days, we were almost blinded.

But with the light, we breathed fresh air, our lungs filling up. And then there was a strange odour that I'd never, never smelled. Not the odour of the cattle train – it was something else. And I saw smoke. My little brother said, 'I can't find my shoe.' I told him, 'You must be more orderly.' And then

the SS came and shouted, '*Los, los!*', which I quickly learned means, 'Fast, fast, come on!' Fast. fast. I saw this German hitting my brother because he wasn't fast enough. A child, a sweet, wonderful little boy who couldn't find his shoe.

Then we saw a lot of people running around in striped clothes, with their shaved heads. I said to Edith, 'Edith, you know, they took us to the wrong place. They will come soon and apologise. This is an insane asylum. Someone will apologise.' And Edith said, 'Wherever we are, it can't be as bad as this cattle car.'

Then some people in striped clothing started to speak Yiddish, so we understood that they were inmates of this – whatever this place was that we had come to. They said, 'Hurry up, leave all your luggage, just leave everything.' And we said, 'But how

Selection of Hungarian Jews in Auschwitz-Birkenau, German-occupied Poland, spring 1944.

Josef Mengele, former physician at Auschwitz-Birkenau. Known as 'the Angel of Death', he oversaw human experimentation and Selektions, where those unfit for labour were removed from the prison population to be killed.

will we find it all?' 'Don't worry about it. Hurry. Line up in fives, and the faster you go the less punishment you'll get. Just move fast.' And they said to the mothers, 'Tell the children not to cry, because if they don't they'll get some water.' And so every mother said to her child, 'Shh, don't cry, they'll give you some water.' And that is why we went passively into Auschwitz. Because what mother would jeopardise her child getting some water?

They pointed the women with little children aside, so Mother, with my brothers and Grandfather were in one line, and Edith and I were in the other. A tall, impressive-looking soldier stopped me and asked, *'Haben Sie Kinder?'* Do you have

children? I stretched and smiled. 'I'm only fifteen,' I replied in German. He motioned me in another direction, separating me from Edith. Later, I found out this was Dr Mengele. I saw him many times. He experimented on people, either people who were unusually tall, as I was, or twins. Sometimes he selected people who had light skin, or who had small hands; sometimes people who had blue eyes. Nobody ever knew what the selection was for. But he was called 'the Angel of Death', because in his hands were the lives of countless people. It took only seconds to select whether someone got life or death. Absolutely immaculate in his uniform, his boots shiny. And here we had come down from this cattle car, unwashed, thirsty. And he, as if listening to music, conducted with his baton: life, death, life, death. Seconds. It took him just seconds.

Edith and I were separated.

They took me to a place, where I had to undress for a shower and they took our clothes from us. Afterwards you got somebody else's dress. I got a long black shiny evening dress that was three times my size. It could be wrapped right around me.

I kept asking, 'When can I see my mother?' I went over to the SS woman, not knowing that in Auschwitz you cannot address an SS guard, and said, 'Where is my mother?' She slapped my face and said, 'You don't talk about mothers here!' That was my welcome to Auschwitz, and also my first lesson: don't ask questions and don't talk to the SS.

They took us to Birkenau, to the C Lager, into a barrack. There were thirty-two barracks in C Lager, each housing a thousand people. Thirty-two thousand people. The whole area was surrounded by electrified barbed wire fence. That night I had one of my recurring dreams that I am at home, that I'm very cold, because my covers have fallen off, but my father would come soon and cover me. Then I woke up in this terrible place, with one blanket for ten people. We slept on wooden planks, with no pillow, no sheets, nothing. If you wanted to turn over, everybody had to turn over. You couldn't lie on your back, because there would be no room for the others. Three tiers of bunks with ten people each. Every night I dreamed Father came to cover me.

We were woken up by a whistle in the morning when it was still dark outside. We were taken to the latrine, a thousand people at one time. We were taken back to the latrine only one time in twenty-four hours, at night. Everyone had diarrhoea. Accidents were resented by others, who had no choice but to walk in it and sit in it. All that was private in life was negated, your human dignity was violated. The latrine was a place of terror.

Everything – all day and night – had to

Alice Lok Cahana returns with her son to Auschwitz-Birkenau.

be done so fast, and we were not permitted to talk to each other. We had to be silent.

The first night they gave me some bread and a bit – a tiny little bit – of margarine. Because they ran out of shoes they let me keep my own shoes. I took the margarine and shined my shoes with it. I had no idea what starvation was, I was absolutely sure that I would never eat anything like this sawdust bread or the foul soup with wood and straw they gave us that night. I said to someone who stood next to me, 'Do you want this soup. I'm not going to eat this.' And I gave it away. I gave my bread away. The next morning we got coffee, but it wasn't really coffee. By then I was already thirsty and hungry.

On the second day I asked a kapo, 'Where is my mother?' A kapo was a person whom the SS had selected to supervise the prisoners, who had special privileges. She was Jewish, and was there day and night. Nobody could address her, nobody could talk to her, and I approached her and said, 'Where is my mother?' She pointed up, and said, 'There is your mother, and don't ask me this ever again.' I didn't understand. I mean, what is 'There is your mother', and pointing up to the smoke? It was terribly, terribly frightening.

From the first day I tried to find out where they took Edith. Finally someone told me that she had heard that they had taken some Hungarians to B Lager the same day I arrived in C. I also found out that every morning food was taken from C Lager to B Lager before the whistle sounded. After that I got up before the whistle to try to find anyone who could take a message to Edith. I traded a piece of bread for a scrap of paper and managed to have the note taken secretly to B Lager. One day a woman brought me the same piece of paper; on the other side was Edith's handwriting: 'I am coming.' And three days later Edith arrived. We vowed to each other we would never be separated again.

Primitive latrines could be used by prisoners only for a few minutes once before leaving for work and once after work. Auschwitz-Birkenau, 1945.

Alice, holding her mother's prayer book, revisits the latrine where she and her sister Edith celebrated the Sabbath together. Auschwitz-Birkenau

Alice holds a photo of herself taken at the Bergen-Belsen concentration camp just after liberation (see reprint on page 213).

One night Edith and I started to talk about how we used to celebrate the Sabbath at home. We were not allowed to talk, the kapos went back and forth during the night, beating anybody who even whispered, but Edith said, 'Why don't we pray? Why don't we pretend we are at home and that you are setting the table like always?' And we would do this every Friday night, and then we would murmur the Sabbath prayer. And it gave us some kind of normalcy in this abnormal hell we were in.

One Friday we were standing by the latrine when Edith said, 'It's almost Shabbat.' The Sabbath starts when the stars come out. I said, 'Why don't we celebrate inside the latrine? They won't hear us there, we can sing,' because the SS never came in the latrine because it was so horrible. So we ran back to the end and stood in a corner, away from the others, and we started to make our Shabbat ceremony, to sing the Sabbath songs, that are sung every Friday in every Jewish home. And as we sang the melody, other children came around us and started to sing with us. Somebody was from Germany, somebody was from Hungary, Czechoslovakia. And from then on, every Friday night we celebrated the Sabbath in the latrine of Auschwitz. And that gave us hope for another day.

One day I heard a woman talking to

herself as she stood next to me at roll call. In the middle of the night she had given birth to a child that was taken away to the crematorium, and she said, 'If I survive, I will not hate, I will love the world.' She had lost her child, and her blood was still oozing out, and now she was saying she will not hate. And that woman has remained with me all my life. She said, no matter what they do to you, don't hate. How incredible.

Many people got typhoid in Auschwitz. One day Edith said, 'I'm so feverish, I think I also have typhoid.' We were frightened because they always selected the sick people. If they couldn't kill people right away then they took them to the infirmary, where it was just slower death. Edith had to go to the infirmary, and I was frightened again. I went to the infirmary before the whistle in the morning, when only the kapo was there. She said if I gave her my bread I could take the dead people out and go in and see my sister. I was only fifteen, and I had never seen a dead person until I came to Auschwitz. But then I thought, these were people who yesterday walked and talked. They are just like me. So I carried them out, to a pile from where they would be collected, and finally the kapo allowed me to go to see Edith. After repeating this for a couple of days, I went again to Edith and said, 'Pretend you are dead, and I will take you out as a dead

person.' This is how Edith got out of the infirmary, and we were together again.

Often we could hear bombing, but from far away. And every day, people were taken away faster and faster. Selections every day. On October 7, they told the children to line up and they promised us warm clothes. We arrived at a place and were told to take off our clothes and put our shoes in a special pile; we'd be disinfected and would get warm clothes afterwards. I promised Edith I would get her her warm clothes for her birthday the next week, on 14 October. We were taken inside a dark room and they shut the door. We waited and waited and nothing happened. Then the SS opened the door, very angry, and shouted, 'Come out, fast as you can, fast, fast.' The clothes that we had left in a pile were still there. They threw clothes randomly from the pile back at us and hurriedly returned us to the barracks. Later I found out this was the only time that the gas in the crematoria did not work, possibly because of revolt in another crematorium.

Edith and I were selected again, this time to go on a transport. They took us to Guben, to an I.G. Farben ammunitions factory, where we worked. After Christmas the bombing came closer and closer, and rumours began to go around that they were taking us away. Suddenly we were marching through the countryside. Anyone who could not march was shot. Edith became weaker and weaker.

In a place called Gross-Rosen we were taken into a barn for the night. When the whistle sounded in the morning, Edith and I, along with a family named Ibi, pretended not to hear. During the night we had dug a hole and covered ourselves with hay. The SS came back into the dark barn, but they could not find us. Later, on this farm, we found some Italian war refugees who tried to shield us and promised to make us a hiding place in the forest. But before they could do it, an SS soldier discovered us and took us back to the group.

Eventually our group was put on a cattle train to Bergen-Belsen. Bergen-Belsen was the worst hell on earth. It cannot be described in human language. Six days before liberation, they stopped giving us any food whatsoever. Finally someone

Alice and her family after saying the Kaddish prayer for her sister in Bergen-Belsen. Members of the Cahana family (left to right) Alice, Rabbi Moshe, Karen, David being held by Ida, Rina, Tamira, Rabbi Michael and Rabbi Ronny.

Alice Lok Cahana in her studio.

came in and said, 'You are liberated.' I asked Edith what that meant, liberated. She said, 'Free, we are free.' So I got up somehow and went outside to look at freedom before it disappeared. I saw the Red Cross. I could hardly walk. Edith said if we were free 'there must be a hospital. Please take me to a hospital.'

Edith was put in an ambulance. I wanted to stay with her in the hospital, but the soldiers came and said that I had to go back to the barracks. 'But in a few days you will come and you will be together with your sister.' I never found Edith again.

For fifty years I looked for Edith Lok. Recently I got a letter from Bergen-Belsen saying there was nobody on their list named Edith Lok, but they had an Edith Schwarz. And then I remembered that we had decided she would use my mother's name, so that the SS would not try to separate us as family members. Now I am going back to Bergen-Belsen, so my husband can say a prayer with my children and me, and symbolically we will bury Edith Schwarz. But there are a lot of people like me out there, still looking, because for us liberation was not the last day.

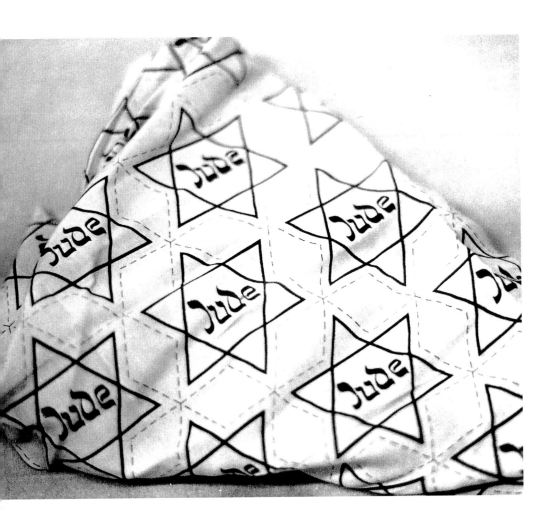

Yellow Stars of David with the word 'Jew' in German printed on a length of material.

Entrance to the ghetto, Munkács, Hungary, spring 1944.

*A young family endures the
intolerable living conditions in
a ghetto in Zalaegerszeg, Hungary,
spring 1944.*

A Jewish couple in the Budapest ghetto wearing Stars of David, January 1945.

A poster warns local residents to stay away from the Jewish ghetto, Munkács, Hungary, spring 1944.

A Jewish man grieves beside the corpses of two women, murdered by the Arrow Cross in a pogrom, Budapest, Hungary, October 1944.

I grew up in a resort town called Polena in the Carpathian mountains; it was a small town, which at that time was part of Hungary. Many people came from all over the country to take the mineral waters, and that was the only time we saw any cars. There were two main streets and we had a post office, a town hall, a church and a synagogue where we had a *cheder* – after-school classes for Jewish children. We had geese and chickens and lived off the vegetables and fruit we grew in our fields, only buying things such as sugar, salt and coffee from the grocery store. Life in that little town was typical of the way Hungarian Jews lived; we didn't have much, but our lives were meaningful and I was happy. I think there were sixty-two Jewish families, a little more than a third of the town's population. Everybody knew each other, shared friends and helped each other. We were six children in my family, and I remember when our cow was pregnant and we ran out of milk my mother would give me this pitcher and I would come home with it full of milk.

As a child I felt that non-Jewish people were our friends. We were orthodox, so they would come to our house and do for us the things Jews were forbidden to do on the Sabbath or on holidays: put out the lights and light candles or our kerosene lamp; we didn't have electricity. In return, my grandfather, whose hobby it was to grow spruce trees, would let his friends and neighbours come and pick a tree at Christmas. I was fascinated by the trees and always wanted one, but my grandfather said, 'We don't celebrate Christmas in our house.' So instead I helped my friends decorate their trees with candy and beans. I thought we were going to be friends for ever, but they soon became my enemies, and I couldn't understand why.

Irene Zisblatt (with vest), with her daughter Robin (with camera), laughs with a childhood friend she had not seen for over fifty years.

Irene in her hometown of Polena (c. 1937)

In 1939, when I was about nine years old, the teacher at my school said that all the Jewish children had to go home as they were no longer welcome in the school. All the non-Jewish children looked at us with such a different look that it made me cry. But the whole Jewish community got together and they arranged for the Jewish children to go to *cheder* to study till curfew, because at the same time we were stopped from going to school, we were also given a curfew: Jewish people were forbidden to leave their houses after six in the evening or before eight in the morning. Then everything began to be taken away from us: businesses, passports.

My father and his cousin gave their business to a gentile, a Hungarian, who agreed that after the war, when we were allowed to have businesses again, he would give it back. Jewish people were sought out and beaten, and Jewish homes were attacked. I remember one Friday, before services were over, I was told to bring back all the prayer books and prayer-shawls from the synagogue. That night the townspeople, many of whom had been our friends, attacked the synagogue with rocks and broke all the beautiful stained-glass windows; a lot of people were hurt.

We didn't see a Nazi in our home town until 1944; everything had been done by the Hungarian police and by local youths under Nazi orders. They sought out and harassed the Jews; people disappeared and we didn't know what had happened to them. Life got harder for us: our food supply was going down and our non-Jewish friends (we had thought they were our friends) weren't helping us because they considered themselves poorer than we were. Two motorcycles was the whole Nazi regime that occupied our town, because the opposition was already there: the people that lived there, who we thought were our friends all these years, turned on us overnight and went with the other side.

My parents never told us anything, but I knew that Poland had been invaded because a lot of Poles crossed over the border. Many of them wanted to escape to Palestine and our rabbi and a group of Jewish people helped them. One night I heard a conversation between my father and another man. He was telling my father what the Nazis were doing in Poland; I'll never forget. He said 'The Nazis are taking our Jewish infants and they're tearing them in half by their legs and they're throwing them in the Dniester,' – that's a river in the Ukraine. I was very scared because I thought they would do that to my younger brother, Luzuro, and when later we were taken from the ghetto on the cattle car to Auschwitz in Poland, I remembered that conversation. But in spite of what we heard from Polish and Slovakian Jews who had escaped, most Hungarian Jews knew absolutely nothing about the Nazi death camps and were convinced that they would somehow survive the war.

Then the Jews were rounded up. As there was a railroad in our town they brought the Jews from the neighbouring towns to our schoolhouse, because from there they could be transported to Munkács – to the ghetto. A lot of people tried to hide in underground bunkers and caves; my father and his brother built double walls in the attic and stored water, dry fruit and bedding there. When attacks by the pro-Nazi *Nyilas* – the Arrow Cross party – increased, we

went into hiding. A friend of my father who was in the Hungarian army sealed up our house from the outside so it looked like nobody was there. In the few weeks we were there I used to go out the back window when it was dark to get a newspaper and food and to find out what was going on. But they broke down our front door and opened up the walls; they knew exactly where we were. They gave us a few minutes to get all our valuables together and marched us out of the house. And our friends, so-called, and neighbours, they were standing along the road yelling, 'It's about time you're going out of here, we don't need any Jews in our town.' I couldn't believe my eyes. These were people I went to school with. We were friends. Why were they so hostile? Why did they hate us all of a sudden? Of course now if you ask them,

The railroad tracks inside the main gate of Auschwitz-Birkenau.

*Irene and her daughter
Robin revisit the site of the
Munkács ghetto.*

'Did you see what was going on?' they all say, 'We didn't see anything.'

We were taken to the ghetto, which consisted of a couple of streets around a brick factory. All the houses were already crammed full when we got there, so we built a little tent from our tablecloths and sheets, whatever we had in our suitcases, and we lived under that. We were fenced off from the city by this big gate. It was a very depressing place, with hardly any green around, just a lot of concrete surrounded by high barbed wire. There were guards everywhere with big German Shepherd dogs on tight leashes. On one side of the ghetto was a river and, across the river, on a high mountain, was a prison with more guards with machine-guns pointing at the ghetto at all times. I have no idea how many people were there but there must have been thousands, because they had been brought from all over the county. Every morning the men and boys were rounded up and taken to work on building the railroad into the ghetto. One day I went to the river to wash some clothes and a guard came up to me and said, 'You're not Jewish, what are you doing in the ghetto?' He offered to take me back to Polena, I think he wanted to save me, but I told him 'I have to be here now because my family is here.' I ran away and told my mother and she didn't send me to the river to wash clothes any more.

It was bad there; we didn't have enough food, though the people in Munkács who were still in their homes and the Red Cross occasionally sent packages – maybe a loaf of bread or a salami, which we shared with as many as a hundred people. It all made me feel confused, lost and very, very sad; I felt I was nothing, a nobody. I couldn't understand why this was happening – we were nice people, we did good things in our lives and my brothers and sisters were so little they couldn't have done any harm to anybody. So why were we being made to suffer like that? I kept asking my mother and grandmother, 'Why are we here and why can't we go home?' They said, 'Well, soon, pretty soon we will go home.' But soon never came. At least we were lucky that the whole family was still together.

And then one day the railroad was finished. The train came in the night and it was announced that everybody who wanted to go to Tokaj to work in the vineyards should get on the train. Everybody went gladly; where we were was hell, and going to work in a vineyard was like going to heaven. We were allowed to take only one suitcase per person, so I wore all the clothes I had. My mother said to me, 'I rolled up diamonds in the hem of your skirt. If you don't have enough to eat, these are to buy bread so you can stay strong and be able to work.' And she told me to say I was twenty years old – I was only thirteen – because then I would be sent to work in a factory where I would get food and I would survive. When we arrived at the railroad station, we realized that we were no going on passenger trains. Cattle cars were waiting for us. My father said, 'They ran out of the other trains, because it's war time.' Anybody who didn't move fast was beaten. When I heard that knock on the outside, like a bolt closing us in there, it wasn't normal any more. I didn't accept that they had run out of the other trains.

We were on that train for about five days; they never opened the doors, they never gave us any water, they never gave us any food. They had one pail for going to the bathroom. The children were screaming, the older people were dying and by the time we got to Birkenau there were several bodies. When the doors were finally opened we saw dogs and men in uniforms with the SS insignia, and they were yelling, 'Dirty Jew, get out of the train!' The men and the boys were stopped at the door and the children and women were pushed down. We were ordered to leave our suitcases by the train, lined up in rows of five and taken into the camp. Then all of a sudden a man wearing white gloves and waving a baton was sending people in different directions. Another uniformed man ordered my mother to put my little

'When we arrived we thought the inmates were sick – and that the chimney was the factory where we were going to work.'

brother down and to let go of my sister and me, but she wouldn't be parted from her children. He got very angry and separated us with his baton, pushing my mother, brother and sister to the left and me to the right – I still have a scar where he hit me. I started to scream and the guard kept pushing me further and further away. I heard my mother say, 'Don't worry, I'll come to see you tomorrow,' her voice fading as we were led off.

We were taken into this big building, like a barrack; there was a huge, huge room inside, separated by benches. We were on one side of the benches and on the other side was a row of Gestapo men and women with their dogs. They ordered us to take our clothes off, but everybody left their underwear on. When they ordered us to take everything off, nobody moved, so they let the dogs loose and they chewed up a couple of people in the front. We all took off our underwear. When they ordered us to take our shoes in one hand and our clothes in the other I suddenly remembered the diamonds. We were told to drop our shoes and our clothes into some bins. At the next section there were women waiting with shears; they didn't shave us but they cut our hair so close that to this day I can feel their scissors on my scalp. I was holding the diamonds and they kept on saying, 'If anybody has any valuables, leave them or

you will be shot.' And I held on the diamonds for dear life. They ordered us to take our shoes in one hand and our clothes in the other hand. I grabbed my blue skirt and, in the crowd, fast, I just took out the diamonds and held them in my hands. I had no clothes on my body, so I put them in my mouth. And then when I walked up again I saw they were opening up people's mouths and looking. I couldn't give them up because I would be shot: why didn't I leave them before? I didn't know what to do, so I swallowed them.

After our shower we were given a pair of wooden shoes and one piece of clothing each – I had a man's pyjama top – and made to look at ourselves in a huge mirror. I think that was the start of making us lose our identity, of the dehumanization process – it's easier to kill a nothing than a somebody. I drew a picture of that first scene in the camp the night after I was liberated: the inmates on the inside with no hair; the people coming in from the trains with their suitcases and hats, looking normal; and the people behind the barbed wire yelling, 'Please, throw us your clothes, throw us your food.' When we arrived we thought the inmates were sick and they were being kept there until they got well – and that the chimney was the factory where we were going to work. Little did I know that I would soon look like them too.

A grate in one of the tiny dungeons in Block 10 of Auschwitz – a site of human experiments.

The doorway to a dungeon of Block 10, Auschwitz.

One day I saw a truck, and heard screaming and I saw two children fall out of the truck. The truck stopped and I saw an SS man pick up the children, bang them against the side of the vehicle and throw them, bleeding, back into the truck. That's when I stopped talking to God.

Many people couldn't endure the pain, the conditions: the hunger, the lice as big as my fingernail embedded into our bodies. When the electricity went on they ran to the barbed wire to commit suicide. Then we were punished. For every man that ran to the wire, they took 100 inmates and killed them in front of us as an example. They didn't even let us die when we wanted. And then I thought, they took away my parents, they took away my identity, they took away my siblings, they took away my possessions. There is something they want from me. And then I thought of my soul. And I decided right then and there, I'm going to get up from this mud and I'm going to fight, because I'm not going to become ashes.

At the twice-daily roll calls selections for the gas chambers and for experiments were made. I went through four experiments. The first time Mengele examined our naked bodies to make sure we didn't have any blemishes before five of us were taken to Auschwitz, next to Birkenau, and had drops put in our eyes. We were then put in

They put us into our new home: one windowless barrack for a thousand people, bunks, three-stories high with ten people to a bunk. All the food we were given was a bucket of soup per barrack. We were completely cut off from the outside world; we didn't know what time it was, we didn't even know what month it was. But somehow we sensed when it was the Day of Atonement, the time for fasting and mourning the dead. And God knows there were plenty of dead. On that day they doubled our rations, and when they found we weren't eating, they gave us nothing for the next five days.

a dungeon, like a tiny cubicle, where we were standing in water up to our ankles; with the door closed it was pitch dark. I don't know how long we were in there – three days, five days or one day, or perhaps one hour – it seemed like forever. They never opened the door and they never gave us anything to eat or drink, so we drank the water we stood in. We went to the bathroom in the water we stood in. Then they took us out and examined our eyes and took us back to the barracks; some couldn't see for several days after. We found out later that they were trying to change the colour of our eyes. The next day I was chosen to work in a section of the camp called 'Canada', because, like the country, it had an abundance of everything. Here all the possessions everyone had arrived with were collected together – clothes, jewellery, candlesticks – and shipped to Germany. There was so much there, while all around us people were dying of hunger and thirst. A few days later I was selected again for another experiment. This time they strapped us to a rusty, dirty table, injected something into the numbers tattooed on our arms and began to cut, without anaesthetic. Half of the time we didn't know what they were doing because we were unconscious from the pain. There was a nurse there and she was filling out papers and keeping records.

Afterwards the nurse – who was Jewish – was told to give us a lethal injection, but she saved our lives by putting us in the tuberculosis room – she knew that the doctors and Gestapo would not go in there because it was contagious – and then taking us to a different barrack so we wouldn't be recognised.

What happened was so horrible, so inhumane, that many survivors just block it out. After 50 years I chose to go back. I needed to go back and talk about what had happened because I felt the world really doesn't know. For fifty years I never read anything about the Holocaust, and among other survivors I never discussed the Holocaust; my own pain is enough to deal with, I certainly didn't need anybody else's. So we got together only for happy things. I

The electrified barbed-wire fence surrounding Auschwitz-Birkenau. Prisoners unwilling or unable to cope with conditions committed suicide by running into the fence.

can't deal with funerals because my loved ones – my parents and siblings – were gassed and burnt in the crematorium; they never had a funeral, so there is no place I can go to remember them. When I went back to Birkenau for the first time in 1994, I still wasn't talking about it, but when I got to the camp I saw it as it was in 1944; not just a chimney here and there, like it is now, or barbed wire, or barracks – I saw it as it had been then: functioning. I relived the march of the 6,000 children who came off the train and went straight to the gas chamber; I saw again the naked gypsies. I was also naked, and one of the gypsies was holding my hand because I was on my own. But I was struggling so hard not to go in there and I hung on at the doorway and, luckily for me, the gas chamber was so overcrowded that when they ordered the guard to close the door so they could release the Zyklon-B gas, I was in the way. The guard grabbed me and threw me out before closing the door. I hid under the roof of the underground crematorium because I knew that I would have to go in with the next transport that came in. I heard the screams and the begging and the gypsies were talking to God like God was there, but He wasn't going to help them. You know, they even had coat hangers by the door to the gas chambers for us so we would think we were going to take a shower and come back to our clothes. As soon as it became quiet, the Gestapo left and a crew of *Sonderkommandos* came, took the bodies from the gas chamber and burnt them. I could still smell the gas from the previous transport, mingling with the stench of the burning bodies which was always there. This is one of the memories that I'll take to my grave.

The whole time I was in the camp, every time I was selected for an experiment, I swallowed the diamonds. I never had the opportunity to buy bread, but I was hoping,

Members of a governmental inspection commission examining sacks of hair from murdered female prisoners, Auschwitz, May 1945.

maybe tomorrow, maybe the next day. They were the only thing I had of my mother's, so it was like holding my mother in my arms. We were allowed to go to the latrine once a day, but I never sat on the hole because I had to find my diamonds. One day an SS woman walked by the door and saw me sitting in the corner. I already had the diamonds in my hand. Usually I would rinse them off in the mud, or in the soup we were given, but there was no time for that, so I swallowed them before she came over and pushed my face into the waste.

So yes, the diamonds were in my body on the death march. When the war was nearing its end, the Nazis took people from the camps, away from the approaching Allies, towards Bergen-Belsen. The death

Those unable to keep pace with the death marches were simply shot and left by the roadside. Outside Auschwitz, 1945.

Irene Zisblatt gives testimony to the Shoah Foundation.

and took out his dog tag and on the dog tag he had a *mezuzah*. I did not think there were any Jews left alive, and when I saw that I just clung to him and tried to kiss the *mezuzah*. They were American soldiers, the most beautiful present from the world and for the first time I acknowledged God again. When they asked me what I wanted to eat I said, 'I just want to have a whole loaf of bread and not have to share it with forty people.' I was fourteen and must have weighed about 40 pounds.

In 1994 I went to the Number II gas chamber where my whole family had been gassed, and I placed a plaque and candles there in memory. I imagined I saw my whole family again, at the *Seder* table, and there was an empty chair at the table which I knew was my chair and I knew that my grandfather would not begin the *Seder* until everybody was sitting at the table. I started to walk towards my chair but my mother said, 'You can't sit in that chair, not yet, you have a lot of things to do before you come to sit in this chair. I want you to promise not to cry any more for me.'

I scraped up the ashes that were still there, and took little pebbles to represent a tombstone for every member of my family that perished there, and I took them to Israel to be buried. Now I feel that they aren't in Auschwitz any more. But when I returned in 1996 I imagined I saw my

march was in the winter of 1945, and those who couldn't keep pace were simply shot by the wayside; if anybody tried to run away they were also shot on the spot. It was cold and snowing, we had no food and no clothes, but some people had blankets which we tore up and used to wrap our feet. I escaped when we were seventeen kilometres from our destination – which was a camp with gas chambers. The SS by then had no ammunition, and also no flashlights, so some of us were able to run away when it got dark. We found one potato and shared it and fell asleep until we were woken up by someone prodding us with a rifle. We saw these big tall people, but we couldn't understand what they were saying. There were just two of them, and then one of them opened up his shirt little four-and-a-half-year-old sister and she was crying because she was cold. Then my daughter asked my permission for her daughter to be *bat-mitzvahed* together with my sister, and it touched me so deeply that somebody would want to have this ceremony for their child with a child who is not alive. Celebrating a *bat-mitzvah* for a child who perished in Auschwitz is something that makes me feel great, because I feel that now my sister will always be remembered.

I think my father's business is now owned by the Ukrainian government, and I don't have a legal or even a moral right to any part of it, but I would like to have something that was valuable to my parents and grandparents – maybe a candlestick or a prayer-shawl. I love my town and I see it picturesque and happy. I was there for the first time since I left in 1944. I was asked in a very nice way, 'Am I planning to take my property and come back to live there?' I said, 'No, I just want my children to know where I come from and I wanted to see my town where I grew up one more time before I die.' A school friend of mine also went back a couple of years ago but the people who now live in her house were not the people that we knew from before the war. She wanted to see what the house looked like inside, but they wouldn't let her in, and said, 'I see Hitler left enough of you

to come back and reclaim your properties.'

A lot of things I still have to keep to myself because they're too horrible to discuss. In fact, for fifty years I was married to a man who knew about the Holocaust, but I don't think he knew how much I was hurting. But not a day goes by that I don't think of my family. There is always something happening in my life that reminds me of certain things. Today is my father's birthday, and I have a *Yahrzeit* (memorial) candle at the house; he was born in 1908, so he would have been ninety today. He and my two younger brothers, they were eleven and nine when they died, went straight to the gas chamber. I survived because I was helped by other people, like the nurse, and the boy who gave me his jacket when I was hiding under the crematorium roof.

I saved the diamonds, all the way through everything. Ten years after the war, when I was in the United States, I had them mounted into a teardrop-shaped pendant, because every time I had to save them, I cried so much. So that tears are appropriate. I have told my children that these diamonds are only to buy bread and they should sell them only if, God forbid, anybody needs food to survive. Otherwise they should be handed down from generation to generation, to the first-born girl in the family forever.

The teardrop pendant made of the diamonds given to Irene by her mother before their deportation from the ghetto.

Hungarian Jews are forced into cattle cars and deported to concentration camps.
Above: Balatonfüred, Hungary, 1944. Right: Soltvadkert, Hungary, 1944.

Deportation at the railroad station of Köszeg, Hungary, May 1944. Women, children and the elderly await a train while behind them a van filled with trunks and other suitcases is loaded.

Hungarian gendarmes supervise the final stages of the loading of a deportation train in Köszeg, Hungary, bound for Auschwitz, May 1944.

Left: After selection in Auschwitz-Birkenau, a group of Jews is brought to Crematoria IV and V along the road between the BIIc camp and the BIId camp, 1944.

Top and right: Preparations for Selektion of Hungarian Jews in Auschwitz-Birkenau, separating the healthy and strong from the sick, the elderly and the very young, 1944.

Hungarian Jews de-train upon arrival in Auschwitz-Birkenau, June 1944.

The woman and the children have been 'selected' out and are walking toward Crematoria IV and V, where they will be gassed. Auschwitz-Birkenau, 1944.

Many Hungarians had never heard of Auschwitz until they arrived. None knew that their future was either slavery or death. Auschwitz-Birkenau, 1944.

'They took my parents, they took away my
identity, they took away all my siblings,
they took away my possessions …
They're not going to take my soul.'

Irene Zisblatt

'By the time my sister and I were
processed into the camp, my mother was
no longer alive.'

Renée Firestone

BILL BASCH

Szaszovo (Tiszaszászfalu) was a small Ruthenian village in the Carpathian Mountains. It was a farming community of about 3,000 gentiles, mostly Greek Orthodox peasants, and about thirty-five to forty Jewish families. I lived with my parents, two older brothers and two younger sisters, and my mother's uncle and aunt who had adopted her when she was orphaned at the age of four. My father had the largest store in the village, consisting of a general grocery, liquor store and a lumber yard, so we were a focal point of the community, providing all the local needs. We had quite a bit of land, too, but because my father was so busy, he gave it out to ten families and at harvest time everything was shared. As most people were illiterate, my father acted as interpreter and signatory for the community's official documents. We also had the village's only radio so, on Sunday mornings, as the gentiles came out of Church, we would open our windows; sometimes as many as 300 people would sit around the house, listening to the Budapest station. My family was respected as the source of strength in that little village, especially as my father and the priest were intimate friends.

We had a small *Schul* but we were too few to support a rabbi, though we did have a *Shochet* to perform the ritual slaughter of animals. There was a biblical tradition that, if there are three sons in the family, the youngest should study the Torah; whilst not fanatically religious, this was my father's dream – that I should become a rabbi. But things did not turn out that way …

My life then was bittersweet; a wonderful, traditional life around the

The arrest of a Jewish resistance fighter by Hungarian police in Budapest, December 1944.

Bill Basch returns with his son Martin to the Dachau concenration camp, Germany.

Temple and a great deal of love from my parents. But when we stepped outside that world, we felt antisemitism all around us. It was inbred in the local children who still believed that we had killed Jesus and that we killed children and drank their blood - we didn't dare show our faces during Easter. At other times, it was very common for kids to throw rocks at Jews in the streets and to shout 'Jew, go to Palestine, you don't belong here.' So, yes, we were needed, respected, but not loved and I was constantly reminded that I'm different. Already in 1939 there were instances in remote villages where Jews were beaten whilst the Hungarian soldiers just stood by, but it was not yet organised antisemitism and we knew it was much worse in Poland where Jews lived in isolated communities and suffered pogroms. But by 1940 news

had filtered down to us that Polish Jews were being taken from their homes and gathered into ghettos, but we children were protected from the horror stories and later we did not know that they were being taken to annihilation camps.

In that same year, however, we started to feel the pressure too; a number of laws started coming through – one of which was that Jews may not own any stores. When more and more laws and orders were imposed, suppressing Jewish business activities, my father told us that he had to close our store and sell the merchandise to a gentile. From the end of 1940 while all gentiles of military age had to report to the military, all Jews of military age had to report for forced labour. At first, the men were still allowed home every few months and my father carried on a small business buying and selling lumber. But then the restriction became total and we had no way of making a living. So my father sold home-made wine and raised angora rabbits for the wool; it was quite a come-down for him.

By 1942 we had became fully aware of the problem, and when my father failed to get American visas for the family, he made a momentous decision. It was during the Passover meal that, with tears in his eyes, he told us that he was afraid that this was the last *Seder* we would spend together and he had therefore decided that the family must split up; that the girls were too young to leave but that the boys should go to different cities. In that way he hoped that some of us would survive. So in the autumn of 1942, when I was fifteen, my mother took me to Budapest to work as an apprentice, without pay or food and only a cutting table for a bed. I survived like that for several months, relying on relatives and acquaintances to provide me with some food.

More than fifty years later, Bill, with his son, walks inside the barbed-wire fence of Dachau.

As things got worse, I discovered that even in Budapest Jews and gentiles didn't mix freely. By then Jews were forced to work at labour camps and, gradually, our freedom was curtailed and the pressure built up. I had had no contact with my family for some time but then I received a postcard from my mother which I remember read: 'Dear Son, we have been repatriated by the German government. We live on a farm. We are doing farm work now, but we are together and we are okay. So don't worry.' The Germans hadn't wanted the Jews in Budapest to know about Auschwitz so they had pre-printed postcards which my mother had to sign and

Bill Basch and his son at Dachau. The Hebrew word on the wall in the background is 'Yizkor', which means 'Remember'.

address in her own handwriting. I wanted to believe that they were together and alive, but by then I already had my doubts; it's amazing how the desire to believe the impossible, to refuse to acknowledge the terrible truth, will sometimes make us accept the lies. Only later did I learn that they had been taken to a brickyard in the city of Nagyszőllős (Sevluš in Czech, now Vinogradov, Ukraine) and from there deported to Auschwitz.

We had already heard about the extermination camps because of the arrival of Polish kids, many of whom had escaped from the Warsaw ghetto. They had nowhere to go – only to Budapest – so there were thousands of young Poles in the city. By that time I had already joined the underground and we did whatever we could to help them get out to Romania. From there, with the assistance of a number of Jewish organisations, we had tried to get them out to Palestine. Unfortunately, out of the several ships that my group were involved with only two made it; from what we heard, three of them sank and two of them were torpedoed. I was supposed to get on the last ship because I was working with this organisation, but because I was fluent in Hungarian, knew my way around and was able to deliver false certificates, the organisation asked me to stay on a little longer. And then it was too late; Horthy was forced to relinquish power and the Nazis arrived in Budapest; and that was the year, 1944, that Raoul Wallenberg came to Budapest and I started working for him.

We had already started printing false papers, in a printing shop which used to be a Jewish gymnasium, but we became really well organised after his arrival. Of course, Wallenberg couldn't have done what he did by himself; he had hundreds and hundreds of young helpers – most of them, like me, no more than sixteen years old. Our main job was to duplicate any papers that Wallenberg's office issued. The copies looked very authentic and we were able to distribute them to people who could not receive these directly from the Wallenberg organisation. With some money donated by wealthy Jews, Wallenberg was able to buy large houses, most of them built around a central courtyard. Once belonging to deported Jews, Wallenberg bought them cheaply from the German government, put up a Swedish flag and housed many people in them. Within my group of several hundred people, my activities were limited to two things: the printing and the delivery of the papers. I spoke Hungarian, knew the city well and had figured out the sewer system; I also had gentile papers in case I was stopped. But if I was stopped and searched, then it

was an instant death sentence. Because there were always guards at the entrances to these protected buildings, we used the sewer system because these houses had huge sewer outlets in the centre of the courtyard. I knew my way around, and once I had delivered food and passports we were able to sneak groups of people out and over the border. Mostly, it was the young Poles who escaped in this way – they were the first ones we were concerned with because they didn't speak Hungarian and it was very difficult for them to move around.

Wallenberg would occasionally come to one of these houses to offer encouragement, but I didn't want him to know who we were or what exactly we did – we didn't want to expose him to the fact that our organisation duplicated the passports and papers he issued – why burden him with that? But of course he knew all along how many passports he himself had issued; he was a very kind and compassionate person. There were other diplomats who tried to help, but no-one succeeded like Wallenberg – they were not so dedicated and the Germans did not have the same respect for them.

I was just a kid, but I had volunteered for this mission and although fear was a constant, I think that by that time I was beyond fear; when you know that you're going to get killed if you are caught,

Jews line up in front of the 'Glass House', the annex of the Swiss Legation at 29 Vadász Street, trying to obtain 'Protective Passes', autumn 1944.

something strange happens – you learn to function despite the danger. It's like the Warsaw ghetto fighters – they knew that they were going to die and were afraid but it didn't stop them from sacrificing their life for a cause. People did whatever they could to survive; this was my choice. I had left the place my mother had found me so I slept in different places knowing that discovery meant instant execution; the method was to take you to the Danube – already flooded with bodies – tie one hand to a second prisoner and to shoot one guy in the back and throw both into the river. Fortunately for me a group of us – close friends – discovered that the Germans had permitted the universities to continue to function and, thanks to the caretaker, whom we paid, the safest sleeping place for us was the university morgue. So for many months I slept on slabs with dead bodies which the university students had used for dissection and research. Of this group, one is now in Israel and another was on TV recently confronting some skin heads who claimed that there had never been a Holocaust. After that show, he learned that one of his brothers had survived and was living in Yugoslavia.

I had been delivering forged papers for a few months when I ran into very serious trouble. Until then I had been very fortunate and escaped capture each time I

was cornered. It was early November 1944 and I was delivering a packet of papers to one of the houses, close to the Danube. But this time, I made a mistake and instead of coming up through the sewer in the middle of the courtyard, I came out in front of the building. I tried to go back but one of the Hungarian soldiers had grabbed me by the neck, pulled me out and started to search my pockets. He found about seven false documents and another one with my picture on it stating that I am a gentile. What was worse, he found a letter that a young man had written to his mother and had begged me to deliver to her in that house. I hadn't read the letter, but the soldier did; it said that within a matter of days the Russians would be outside the city, that the Hungarians and Germans would all be killed and the city liberated. The soldiers started to laugh and joke about 'whose pigeon' I was going to be – it was just a question of minutes before I would be handcuffed and taken to the Danube to be shot; I knew I had to act quickly. They had placed their long, old-fashioned guns against the wall in order to examine all the documents I was carrying; in the few seconds I had to think, I kicked their weapons as hard as I could and started running. It took them some ten – maybe fifteen – seconds to recover their guns and to start shooting at me – I heard

Raoul Wallenberg in his office at the Swedish legation in Budapest, Hungary, winter 1944–5. (See Wallenberg on page 124.)

bullets flying past. Running as fast as I could, crossing the street back and forth, I saw there were Hungarian soldiers marching some 75 Jews down the street. Not knowing where they were taking them, I mingled with them, literally marching past the two soldiers chasing me. Within a few minutes two trucks pulled up, the backs opened up and about forty SS soldiers jumped out and surrounded the group. Because I had escaped so many times before, I though I'd escape one more time, but I knew that this time I would be shot if I moved out of line. Then I found myself on the railroad tracks, being pushed onto a train; this group of Jews was not being taken to another ghetto.

I didn't know whether the train was bound for, Germany or Poland. We wound up five days later in Buchenwald. By that time Poland was half liberated and the Soviet forces, having reached the outskirts of Budapest, were bombarding the city day and night; by January 1945 they were in Budapest. So we were taken to Buchenwald because the Germans needed more labour – they had killed so many that they were running out of people to do certain jobs for them. Of course, I knew nothing of this, or where we were going. Of all the experiences I had – and each person has their own harrowing story to tell – that train journey was probably the most horrible. The journey took days – totally without any food or water. We must have been over 100 people in that cattle car. One of the most horrible things was the stench – people had died, children were screaming and there were women giving birth and having to kill their babies because they knew that annihilation awaited most of them. Three of us tried to escape from a tiny window which was just big enough for a body to squeeze through; the first one to jump fell to his death into a ravine; the second guy had his head shot off, so I got discouraged and decided not to jump; days later we arrived at Buchenwald.

After we unloaded all the dead – maybe 20 per cent, maybe more – they brought us into the camp. I'll never forget; it was a very cold winter night in November. The first thing they did was to undress us and take every possession we had – every little thing like a picture or a key – everything – and then they left us, standing naked, for hours. There is nothing as demoralising and dehumanising as standing in the nude – men and women together – and not knowing what would happen next. People were freezing, screaming and collapsing. Finally, they took us to a room where there was a huge tub with some kind of solution. With two Germans standing by, one by one we had to go through that tub and be dunked in for about a second or two – and it was burning. Thoroughly soaked, we had to stand and wait again in the nude. Several hours passed and we were taken to look into one of the barracks where we saw thousands of people huddled together on the floor – and we were praying to God that we might have the opportunity to get into that barrack, to be allowed to sit on the floor and huddle together for warmth; it was a long, long time before, finally, we were given one of those pyjama-type striped outfits and marched into a barrack.

Two days after that ordeal they called for volunteers to work on the railroads. I had no idea why, but while I was in this barrack for a couple of days, people had said to me 'Kid, no matter what you do, no matter what they ask of you, as long as they offer you work – go and work because if you don't work, they'll kill you.' So I volunteered and told them that I had worked on the railroad in Budapest when I was in the forced labour camp. They collected about 500 of us and put us into cattle cars again – forty-eight in each car – and announced that we would be known as members of the 10th German Eisenbahn Brigade. It sounds fancy, but what it really meant was that – as the Americans were by now constantly bombarding the railroads – these 'brigades', together with German guards and equipment, would arrive to fix the damaged railroads. At first, it sounded good because they gave us enough food to survive, though we never knew when or where they would take us. We would stop somewhere and the Germans would get out, set up their machine guns and dogs and start screaming '*Raus*, out,' as they opened up the cattle cars, and we would have to dig foxholes alongside the railway. Then, while the Germans went into these foxholes, we would be working, sometimes day and night, to fix the damage.

We were never far from the front lines and the Americans bombed these railroads to prevent ammunition and equipment getting through. At the same time we were constantly in danger of being shot by the

Germans and if anyone was injured they would be taken away; we would hear machine-gun fire and we all knew what that meant. Even if we survived the Germans, we were in danger from the Americans who flew reconnaissance planes to see whether their mission had been successful. They came down quite low and could see us fixing the railroads that some fliers had risked their lives to bomb; I think half of us were killed by Americans. I don't know whether they knew that we were Jewish prisoners, but I can understand that their main concern was winning the war, not a few hundred Holocaust survivors. I did this work from December 1944 to March 1945, by which time there were only about forty of us left and the SS made the decision to execute us all. But some soldiers made a deal with the SS that they would take over our group and march us into a camp; not because they were good, but because, knowing that the war was nearly lost, they wanted us to testify that they had saved our lives.

During that march about 20 per cent of the people died or were killed; for years I was haunted by a couple of events from that time. There were three of us friends that were together up to that point. And we swore that we would sacrifice our lives for each other – that we would never let each other down. Kids, you know – we had this sort of a dream that it would be possible. One of the three had an injury in his knee and had gangrene. One of the soldiers noticed him limping, so he comes up and he wants to shoot him. But we step in front of him. He puts down his Luger and he says, 'I give you three seconds, a count to three. Either you let him go or you all die.' Can you imagine, being so young, that decision we had to make? Here, we promised that we will die for each other. But we couldn't keep that promise under threat of death. We did let him down. I've learned one thing from that horrible experience, I could never say 'I'll never do this' or 'I'll never do that'; when you are faced with death you do what you have to in order to survive.

We had another experience, and this is when I learned not to condemn the world – not even the Germans. As we were marching through a small village an elderly woman appeared on the second floor of a house. I can see her now; she held her apron up and stood against the window. We were starving and used to people throwing rocks or hot water at us, but when she dropped the apron, twenty loaves of bread just rolled onto the street right next to us. Of course, we rushed to get at the bread – we did not see the SS soldier who aimed his machine gun and shot her. This woman gave her life for us,

Bill with his son looking at the wooden bunks in a barracks at the Dachau concentration camp, Germany.

so how can I hate every German? Finally, after ten torturous days, in the third week of April 1945, we reached our destination – Dachau.

During the time I was at Dachau there were more terrible experiences. One of the hot commodities in the camp was potato chips, made from potato peels, which some of the old-timers were willing to barter for what they described as 'a slice of beef'; later we found out that there was no cattle – it was human flesh – so, without knowing it, I had participated in cannibalism. Even if subconsciously we might have suspected something, we couldn't remain moral because survival was everything and those that survived were those who were prepared to break the

moral code. Another story; we slept in bins – filthy, full of lice, four of us with one thin blanket between us. It was freezing cold and many times I woke up when I realised that the man next to me was not warming me because he was dead. But it didn't move me; there was no crying, no emotion. All I did was to ask the guy next to me to help me dump the dead man onto the floor – now we had the blanket between just three of us and we could hope to survive another night. So no, I couldn't afford to become morally or emotionally involved with other people; I never killed anyone, but neither did I cry for anybody in the camp.

We did not know then that this would be the first camp that Eisenhower's forces

'We couldn't remain moral because survival was everything, and those
that survived were those who were prepared to break the moral code.'

*Inmates from Dachau during a
death march, spring 1945.*

would liberate. But when the Germans realised this, we became aware that they were wiring up the whole place with explosives. But, early on the morning of 29 April, we heard gun shots and explosions. For a moment we thought the camp was being exploded, but it was the Americans marching in, totally unexpected, and catching the Germans off-guard. The scene that followed was unbelievable; people literally tore some of the Germans apart; that was the day that I, along with some 29,000 other prisoners, was finally liberated.

After the war some people went completely crazy and killed themselves; many others died from typhoid fever and a week or so after I was liberated I just collapsed on the street. The first thing I remember was waking up – after fifteen days had elapsed – and seeing what I thought were clouds; I imagined that I had died and was floating on a cloud. When I was able to focus I saw a nurse sitting next to me; it was 4 June and I was in an American field hospital . The nurse told me that, because there were so many survivors, those not expected to live had been laid out on tables until they died and could be buried. For some reason I survived, so they brought me back into the field hospital and revived me – bald, full of lice – but I made it.

When I recovered I returned to Budapest to search for my family. For a week I couldn't find anyone; finally I discovered, through Jewish agencies, that someone had seen my sister in Bucharest and she had heard that I was looking for her. My sister had been given some money to help her start her life again and she was coming to Budapest to look for me – I was en route to Bucharest to find her! So instead I returned home to my little town and planned to leave a notice at the railroads to let her know that I was at our house. But when I arrived at the railroad, two Jewish kids grabbed me and brought me to the home of one of my distant relatives; They told me my house had been taken over by seven gentile families and that other survivors who had tried to return to their homes had been killed. Having come through the war, I was now afraid to be killed in my own village. At my relative's house I found bedding, grain and food; this was my relative's last contribution to the survivors of the Holocaust – he committed suicide by hanging himself because he could not cope with what he had experienced. That is how some people 'coped'. I stayed there for several days until my sister finally came and we made the decision to leave Hungary.

Not knowing if anybody had survived, it was a joy to see my sister. We waited three or four weeks hoping someone else might show up – when no-one else came we assumed that they were all dead. We didn't know that my brother Ted had survived until we got to Italy – a year or so later. Before then my sister and I spent some time in Austria and experienced displaced persons camps; they were not the horrible experiences we had had in the concentration camp, but they were very sad places. We wound up in Italy in a displaced persons camp near Rome and, while we waited to go to Palestine we organised a kibbutz-style life, sharing our few belongings. It was in Italy that I discovered that Ted was alive, but the night I arrived, having finally traced him to another DP camp, I was told that he had been one of the 500 kids allowed to go to Palestine and that he had left the day before. My brother wound up fighting for the establishment of the State of Israel and it was some six or seven years later that we all got together in America, where my brother then decided to settle.

As for me, I arrived in Los Angeles on 21 November 1947 and started work the following day in a cleaning store, shortening trousers. My first goal was to learn English so I went to night school; there I met a young lady, also a Holocaust survivor from Czechoslovakia. She was very sweet and we were married two years later and had a son and two daughters. Rose – or Holly as she was called – and I were married for forty-seven years, but hers was a very sad story because she developed an unidentified illness. After years of sickness and surgery the University of Oslo, where they did a lot of research on Holocaust survivors, came up with the conclusion that there was no cure because my wife's illness was really due to the poison that they had given her when she was being experimented on as a girl in Auschwitz. Some people had no reaction to this 'concentration camp syndrome', but in her case the interior of her blood vessels began to deteriorate and she died from a haemorrhage after fifteen years of illness. But she gave me three beautiful children, who in turn have given me five gorgeous grandchildren; they are a joy and have fulfilled my life. Economically, I have recovered too; God was with me and helped me and I have been able to retire at the age of 61 to enjoy a traditional Jewish life with my family.

After the Holocaust I did not have the time to think about my faith – the immediate need was for survival. Later, I did question my beliefs – if God is just and merciful how could He have just stood by? It was very painful for me to accept Him unquestioningly, in the way I had when I was a child. So, I compromised – I still believe in God but I'm not as dedicated a Jew as I used to be. When my wife died I suffered again the loss of my parents, so I wrote a six-page letter to my father thanking him for the strength he gave me which helped me to survive the camps. I am haunted by the fact that I do not know where he perished; I've been searching most of my life and heard rumours that he was marched into one of the Polish camps and that he was shot with a group of about 200 others. I've written several times to an international tracing service in Germany, but I still do not know where and how he died. As I grow older, it has become very important to me to have that information.

Presently I am trying to repay to society in some way by going out to schools and lecturing children about the Holocaust – not so much about the atrocities, but about why and how it happened. I try to explain to them what hatred can do and how it can destroy a nation and its people. It's amazing the reaction I get; sometimes I see tears and I have a booklet of letters from these kids, some of them expressing their gratitude for showing them what hatred towards other people does, pledging that they will never hate anyone. So I write back to them and feel I am contributing to something good.

Yes, at the beginning I often asked myself why had I survived and not my parents,

brothers and sister, but I cannot say now that I feel guilty for having had the willpower to survive. Today and now I have a new life; today I'm more interested in what I can do to leave the world a better place after I'm gone.

Bill toasts his family, including two children and five grandchildren. Pictured (right to left) are his son Martin, grandson Maxwell and grandson Abel.

Raoul Wallenberg in his office at the Swedish legation in Budapest, Hungary, 26 November 1944.

WALLENBERG, RAOUL (1912 – 1947?): SWEDISH DIPLOMAT AND RESCUER. RECRUITED BY THE WAR REFUGEE BOARD AS A MEMBER OF THE SWEDISH LEGATION, HE ARRIVED IN BUDAPEST IN JULY 1944. HE RESCUED THOUSANDS, PERHAPS TENS OF THOUSANDS OF HUNGARIAN JEWS BETWEEN JULY–DECEMBER 1944, PRIMARILY THROUGH THE DEVICES OF *SCHUTZ-PÄSSE*, HOSTELS, AND PROTECTED HOUSES. WALLENBERG BOARDED DEPORTATION TRAINS, INTERRUPTED DEATH MARCHES, AND CONVINCED NAZIS THAT JEWS HAD SWEDISH PROTECTION. IN DECEMBER 1944, PRIOR TO THE RUSSIAN OCCUPATION, WALLENBERG PERSUADED AND THREATENED THE *WEHRMACHT* TO PROTECT THE BUDAPEST GHETTO FROM ARROW CROSS DESTRUCTION. HE WAS KIDNAPPED BY THE SOVIETS ON 17 JANUARY 1945. THE FOLLOWING DAY 80,000 JEWS WERE LIBERATED FROM THE BUDAPEST GHETTO. DESPITE NUMEROUS ALLEGED SIGHTINGS, WALLENBERG'S PASSPORT WAS RETURNED TO HIS FAMILY BY MIKHAIL GORBACHEV, WHO INSISTED THE RESCUER WAS DEAD. HE IS THE MOST CELEBRATED RIGHTEOUS GENTILE HONOURED AT *YAD VASHEM*, AND ONE OF ONLY TWO HONORARY CITIZENS OF THE UNITED STATES.

WALLENBERG

SCHUTZ-PASS

Nr. 67/77

Name: Dr. Joseph Katona *Név:*	
Wohnort: Budapest. *Lakás:*	
Geburtsdatum: 2. März, 1909. *Születési ideje:*	
Geburtsort: Zalaegerszeg *Születési helye:*	
Körperlänge: 166 cm. *Magasság:*	
Haarfarbe: schwarz **Augenfarbe:** braun *Hajszín:* *Szemszín:*	**Unterschrift:** *Aláírás:* Katona József

SCHWEDEN SVÉDORSZÁG

Die Kgl. Schwedische Gesandtschaft in Budapest bestätigt, dass der Obengenannte im Rahmen der — von dem Kgl. Schwedischen Aussenministerium autorisierten — Repatriierung nach Schweden reisen wird. Der Betreffende ist auch in einen Kollektivpass eingetragen.

Bis Abreise steht der Obengenannte und seine Wohnung unter dem Schutz der Kgl. Schwedischen Gesandtschaft in Budapest.

Gültigkeit: erlischt 14 Tage nach Einreise nach Schweden.

A budapesti Svéd Kir. Követség igazolja, hogy fentnevezett — a Svéd Kir. Külügyminisztérium által jóváhagyott — repatriálás keretében Svédországba utazik.

Nevezett a kollektiv útlevélben is szerepel.

Elutazásig fentnevezett és lakása a budapesti Svéd Kir. Követség oltalma alatt áll.

Érvényét veszti a Svédországba való megérkezéstől számított tizenegyedik napon.

Reiseberechtigung nur gemeinsam mit dem Kollektivpass. Einreisevisum wird nur in dem Kollektivpass eingetragen.

Budapest, den 15. September 1944

KÖNIGLICH SCHWEDISCHE GESANDTSCHAFT
SVÉD KIRÁLYI KÖVETSÉG

Kgl. Schwedischer Gesandte.

Antiqua Nyomdai és Irodalmi Rt. Budapest
2389 F. Wiesmayer Emil

A Shutz-Pass issued by the Swedish legation of Budapest under the leadership of Raoul Wallenberg.

RENÉE FIRESTONE

You have to know that I was born and raised in Užhorod (Ungvár), the capital of the region; it was small but modern with a cosmopolitan feel. Out of a population of about 32–34,000 maybe one third were Jews. Our home was on the outskirts of the city itself, in an acacia-lined, residential street. On one side of the river which ran through the town there was an old fort under which there were two homes. We lived in one of them; in the other lived a Czech congressman who had a daughter with whom I was friends. Stairs led up to the fort where there was a bakery from where you could always smell fresh bread baking and just next to our house was another Jewish family who had a little gift shop. These were the only businesses in that area. Within the fort was a seminary and a nunnery, as well as a church right next to it, so we used to see the priests and nuns as they passed our house. When my

mother was young she had attended a Catholic elementary school, so all these nuns knew her and they always greeted her.

My father built that home in 1929. It was a big house with a mezzanine on top with a balcony, which was my brother's quarters. Later, my father gave that apartment to a family who couldn't support themselves. It was a lovely villa with a rose garden in the front. The fruit and vegetable garden in the back was my mother's hobby – actually her therapy. My mother suffered from headaches and she had been advised to find an outdoor hobby. She started this fantastic garden where she grew huge tomatoes, weighing around two pounds each. My father was a craftsman and was very artistic; he had a store where he sold textiles and custom-made menswear. Probably my deepest and fondest memories are of my father whom I loved dearly. My brother Frank was five

Renée returns after fifty years to the house where she grew up, Užhorod.

The city of Užhorod (Ungvár), in the region of Carpatho-Ruthenia.

years older and we were very close; he was the same age as my boyfriends so we would go on dates together. My little sister, Klara, was four years younger than me.

Our house was always filled with Jews and non-Jews. We were assimilated and without any prejudices. It was 1938, I was fourteen years old and didn't understand what was going on outside our little town. Yes, I did hear Hitler on the radio yelling about war and about the Jews, blaming them for all the evils in the world. But a child doesn't understand any of that. I do remember, though, that at one point my father, who never used to go to Temple, not even on holidays, all of a sudden began to attend Friday night services and come home with strangers. I realised later that these were refugees coming to Hungary, running away from Poland. On Friday

nights, the men from most of the Jewish families went to Temple to bring these people home and give them shelter until they moved on – mainly to the Soviet Union or to Palestine. That was the first indication I had that really serious things are happening to the Jews. But still, Hitler was in Germany and what happened in Germany didn't reflect on us – we were far away from all that. We just never believed that the Hungarians would do such things – and probably they wouldn't have, had the Germans not eventually occupied Hungary.

On May 4 1939, Jewish children were no longer allowed to attend public school, with the exception of those about to graduate. One day, my brother, who was in the graduating class, didn't return home from school. We didn't know what had happened to him and waited up the whole night. The following day, desperately worried, my mother went to the police department and to the school – nobody knew anything. Finally she hired an attorney, who later asked my father for a large sum of money for the release of my brother. We found out that six Jewish boys were removed from their graduating class and taken to a neighbouring town where they were interrogated, beaten and tortured. When my brother was finally released, he was black and blue all over and would not talk about this experience.

They had accused the boys of being Communists and of disseminating communist pamphlets, but I knew that he had had no political connections. But after graduation he was taken away to a forced labour camp where we were permitted to visit occasionally. I remember going with my mother once to visit him and my Hungarian fiancé, László, who was in the same camp. Some time around 1943, before we were deported, I had become

Renée's family (c. 1934). (Counterclockwise from bottom left) Renée Weinfeld (Firestone), Mother Johanna Rosenfeld Weinfeld (nicknamed Jolly), Father Morris Weinfeld, Unknown, Uncle Joseph Weinfeld, Unknown (Dr Brown's sister), Dr Sándor Brown, Unknown (Dr Brown's mother).

unofficially engaged to this good-looking Hungarian young man, a fencing champion, so I was both excited and frightened – I didn't know what a labour camp was and didn't know what to expect. It was an emotional visit because the boys already knew that they were going to be taken to the Soviet Union front, where the Hungarians were fighting alongside the Germans, so it was a sort of parting. I met a number of other Jewish boys on that visit – including Bernard who was to become my husband – they were all frightened, not knowing what was going to happen to them. As it turned out, they were taken to the Ukraine where they were used as mine sweepers. Many were blown up; those who contacted typhoid, László included, were locked in a barrack which was then set on fire. That is how I lost my fiancé.

We began to hear about Germans herding the Jews behind barbed wire and, later, the stories were getting worse. We began to hear about mass shootings into mass graves. In 1941 there was already a law that those Jews who could not prove that their ancestors – as far back as the eighteenth century – were citizens, had to make themselves known – we found out that they were then deported and dumped over the border into Poland. But as the Poles wouldn't let them in, they were roaming around in no-man's land so the

Germans collected them and shot them into mass graves. I knew of a woman who was shot with her mother and two sisters; she survived because she must have fallen into the grave first and then her mother and sisters fell on top of her. When she crawled from underneath the bodies she was recaptured, raped by nine German soldiers and then left to die. A Polish farmer found her and saved her life.

As long as we were permitted, my father listened to the radio – then that too was taken away from us. People wonder how it is that we didn't do something, that we didn't run away. We didn't hide. One can be clever with hindsight and now I can see that there were definite signs of danger – but not then, living at home with the security of family around you. Things didn't happen at once, it happened very slowly. So each time a new law or restriction came out, we said, 'Well, it's just another thing, it'll blow over.' The fact is that finally, when we knew that they were going to take us away, the war was upon us – we were very close to the Soviet Union and could actually hear the war – so we thought we would be safe, that the Russians would arrive and liberate our town any minute. But they didn't, the Russians went a different direction – towards Poland – and we were trapped.

The next restriction was that a Jew

cannot walk out on the street without a yellow star. We heard that in Germany they had to wear the yellow star before they were taken away, and in Poland they did that, so at that point we were worried. I remember the first time I went out with this star. I'm not sure whether I was embarrassed or scared – I know that I saw a German officer coming towards me and I didn't know whether I should cover it or whether it would be safe to just walk on the street with it. But then I saw a non-Jewish friend of mine coming towards me – not just an acquaintance but a friend who used to be in my house and I in hers almost every day – we were the closest of friends. I was hoping that she would come over to me and embrace me and tell me how sorry she is about what's happening to us but she crossed the street and passed by without even looking at me.

From the time we had to wear the yellow star, the Jews became totally isolated; the curfew meant that we couldn't go out on the street any time we wanted, so it was hard to judge how the people around us felt. One day, posters appeared all over town saying that all Jews would be relocated. It was just after my twentieth birthday and I remember that we were all sitting around the Passover table. We had no ideas where we were to be relocated but there were rumours that we were going to be taken to Germany to work for the Reich. My father tried to reassure us, my sister and me, that they had promised that families would stay together. And my father said, 'As long as we will be together, we will help each other out and everything is going to be all right. You can hear that the war is coming closer and that it is going to be over soon, so don't worry, we'll be back in no time.' Somehow, I trusted that; I believed that that's what was going to happen. They told us that we can pack one suitcase each, weighing no more than 50 kilos, so that everyone can carry their own case. My father was worried that we shouldn't take too much because we might get tired walking. On the other hand, he also worried that we should have warm clothes and a second pair of shoes, in case we stayed away longer than anticipated. He told us, I remember, to take a little bit of sugar and maybe a little food with us. As all the Jews were taken out of their homes and marched out of town, our neighbours were looking out from behind their curtains. I did not know then whether they were sad and couldn't face us or whether they were glad that we were being taken away; later I found out that as soon as we had left they looted our homes. When we were packing, I was very depressed and worried and wanted to take something that would remind me of the good times. I came across a bathing suit

that my father had brought me from a
business trip three years earlier. He always
brought my sister and me something and,
of course, we always asked 'What did you
bring?' He opened this box and out came
the most beautiful swimsuit, made out of a
new stretch fabric with a shiny satin finish
and print of multicoloured flowers. But I
felt it would be silly to pack it so I left it to
one side. Then in the afternoon, when I
heard the soldiers' boots coming up the
stairs, I ran back and put this bathing suit
on under my dress and that's how I left
for the train station to be shipped off to
the camp.

We were told to wait in our homes
with our packed cases. There was a 24-
hour curfew and during that time
they went from house to house, taking
away all the Jews. We didn't think to
question these orders because we had
already heard that this was also happening
in other places. Human nature is such
that you are willing to accept almost
anything as long as you feel that you're
going to survive. We wanted to believe
that they were going to take us to
Germany to work. We really wanted to
believe that; we didn't know that by
then the whole of European Jewry was
already in camps.

We walked all day and into the night
toward the outskirts of our town, not

knowing where they were going to take us,
arriving finally at a location where they told
us to settle down. It was a very dark night –
no moon, no stars – we had no idea where
we were so most of us dozed off sitting on
our cases. It was in the morning when I
realised that we are in a brick factory yard. I
was puzzled when they told us that we are
going to be staying here for a little while –
did they want us to live in this brick yard
without any shelter? I noticed that there
were some bricks drying under an awning
so I put my suitcase there and told my
mother and father that maybe here
we would at least have some sort of roof
over our heads. My mother opened her
suitcase and out came a pure silk down
quilt which she put on this dirty ground.
She lay down on that quilt and fell into a
terrible depression; until we were taken
away from there she never got up and
she only ate if we fed her. We stayed at that
place for about two weeks, fed on some
kind of soup or goulash brought to us from
the city.

By the time I had decided that nothing
could be worse than the conditions we
were in, we again heard rumours that they
were going to take us to Germany. We also
heard terrible stories about people who
had money being taken away and beaten,
some of them to death. I said to my father,
about whom I was very worried, 'Nothing

Renée (right) with a childhood friend at the swimming pool in Užhorod.

can be worse than this, let's try to get on to the first transport. Let's get out of here.' I talked to people, I manipulated and I accomplished what I wanted – we were taken on the first transport.

There's a story that I'm always reminded of when I think of that time. Before the war my father took in a young gentile boy as an apprentice. He was a son of a shoemaker who had nine children and was unable to feed them all. Not only did my father take him on as an apprentice, he also took him into our home and, from the age of thirteen, he grew up with us. When my father's business was taken away from him he turned over everything he had to this boy and told him, 'I don't know what's going to happen to us, if we need anything, we know that we can depend on you, you're like my son.' And the boy cried and promised that he would do anything he could for us. While we were in that brick factory, we were running out of supplies so my father sent a letter to this boy to whom he had left all his possessions; the answer came back that he would not risk his life to help us. This is an example of how our friends – our trusted friends – turned against us overnight. That's why it's so hard to comprehend what really happened. Some fifty years later, we still keep asking ourselves, how could this have happened? What had we

done that made our friends so willing to turn against us?

So, early in the spring of 1944, we were on that first transport. We had no idea where they are taking us, we only believed, and hoped, that we are going to work for the German Reich – maybe in a factory, maybe we'd be harvesting food for German soldiers. All that was fine, as long as the family remained together. I remember, as I was preparing for this journey, my first thought was to put the bathing suit on again because I didn't want anybody to know that it was in my suitcase. We were lined up in the brick factory and taken to the railroad station by the Hungarian soldiers. They wore a very distinctive uniform and were known for their terrible, terrible brutality – sometimes worse than the Nazis. Of course, without that sort of complicity, not only from the Hungarians but also from the Ukrainians, Poles, French, Belgians – without such willingness to collaborate, Hitler would never have accomplished what he did.

When we arrived at the railroad station we realised that we were not going on passenger trains – the cattle cars were waiting for us. We also noticed that the train was guarded by German, not Hungarian soldiers so that sort of gave us a signal that we were going to Germany. They packed so many of us into each wagon – there were about 120 in ours – that there was not enough room for everybody to sit down. We took the elderly and we sat them around the edges of the car so that they could lean back, and we took the little babies and children from their mothers and handed them to the older people. As they didn't give us any food or water before locking the doors, this signalled to us that we can't be going very far. In one corner of our wagon we noticed there was a little straw and in the middle of it there was a bucket – that was to serve as a bathroom for 120 people. I remember, too, that there was a little window but that it was covered with plywood; when the doors were closed the only light seeped in through the cracks.

The journey began in the late afternoon; we travelled through the night, through another day and then stopped the following night. It was total darkness. The light only seeped through the cracks of the cattle car. We heard soldiers shouting at us that if we have any valuables we should hand them over. From outside we could hear screaming and shooting and we were convinced that they were finding some of these things on people and were killing them; it was very, very frightening. I saw young women, who had probably just got married, take off their wedding rings and hand them through the cracks to the

soldiers. Later we found out that this was not part of the rules; these Nazis were looting for themselves. As the train continued, the looting was repeated every night. But there was another reason why the train stopped so frequently; it was because of the number of transports which were being brought in from other directions, all heading for the same

A portrait of Renée Firestone's father, Morris Weinfeld, c. 1914

Renée returns to the Auschwitz concentration camp with an interpreter to trace her family's fate.

seen anything like it – I didn't know whether it was a community or a prison. Later I noticed some skeleton-like humans walking around in striped uniforms so then I thought that it must be some kind of prison – but I still had no idea that this was something unique. I recall that, as we were being marched from the railroad station to the bathhouse I saw, behind some trees, a clearing where people were sitting – mostly elderly and very young – and they were taking off their clothes. I had no idea – I couldn't imagine – what was happening. I didn't tell my sister who was standing next to me. I saw how they were throwing people into these fire pits. I said to myself, 'Something is wrong with me, my mind is going. I can't be seeing soldiers grabbing old people and children and dragging them to this pit.' I couldn't be seeing this. So I wiped the memory out. Years later, after reading an article, I was reminded of what I had seen.

We were taken to an underground dressing room, told we're going to be taking a shower after this horrendous journey and then we'll be assigned to our work. But first, we were given a postcard and told to write to someone we knew in Hungary and to tell them that we were well; I wrote to my brother. They deceived us with everything they said. They told us to be very careful how we fold our

destination. The trains stretched so far back that I could not see where they ended.

When the doors were finally opened I decided that I was going to be the first one off the train because I wanted to get myself a good job; that way, I thought, I could save my 14-year-old sister who was not strong or big enough to work, and my parents, who I thought of as elderly, though they were only forty-two and fifty-two. But when I jumped on to the platform I knew right away that everything they had told us was lies. I could see this huge territory surrounded by barbed wire and every few feet there was a wooden tower with a machine gun pointing at us. I had never belongings; they told us to remember exactly where we put our things because when we come out of the shower we have to dress quickly. But a few minutes later a commando removed all our belongings.

I remember I got undressed with the rest of them and there I was, standing in the bathing suit. I had a premonition, this feeling, that if I take this bathing suit off, if I leave this bathing suit behind, all the wonderful memories that were built in this bathing suit, everything that meant anything in life to me, I'm going to leave behind. Today when I think about that bathing suit I remember that, with that suit, I left behind my family, my friends, my

Renée (centre) with her childhood friend Elizabeth Gottlieb (left) and another young woman (unknown) at the Užhorod pool before the German occupation.

They were throwing people into these fire pits. I said to myself, 'Something is wrong, my mind is going.' I couldn't be seeing this.

Renée lights candles for her family at the ruins of a crematorium at Auschwitz-Birkenau

relatives. Once, after the war, when I told this story to a group of people, I received an envelope containing three pictures of me in that bathing suit – to this day I have no idea where they came from.

After the shower, wet and naked, we were surrounded by Nazi soldiers and vicious dogs, barking and screaming at us; we did not know who was barking the louder. There is something about being stripped of your clothing – you suddenly realise how vulnerable you are. We had to undress in front of the soldiers, this was horrendous for me – a 20-year-old who had never even undressed in front of my father. But on that day we were made to stand outdoors until midnight, by which time the fear was unbearable, and so we waited, wet and naked, until about midnight, and then they finally permitted us to walk into one of these wooden barracks where they shaved our bodies and our heads and sprayed us with pesticide. This was the first time I saw raw brutality. The women didn't know how to line up so the kapos – the overseers – were beating them with wooden bats; many women were bleeding, many never got off the ground.

My mother was selected at the railroad station to go the left, while my sister and I went to the right. My mother was taken straight from the railroad station to the gas chambers. By the time my sister and I were

processed into the camp, my mother was no longer alive. It was only a few days later, at Auschwitz that I found out what this place was all about – when a kapo pointed to the chimney which I hadn't noticed before and asked me whether I could see the smoke and fire coming out of it. This was because I had asked her when we would be reunited with our parents, and she pointed to this chimney and said 'When you go through the chimney you'll be reunited.' I turned to some older prisoners and asked them, 'What does that mean, what is this woman talking about?' Within a few days we had found out that this is one of the extermination camps and that people are brought here to be killed. How do you understand that? I mean, I heard it, but I could not believe that they are going to kill me for nothing. I was to discover later that when we came to Auschwitz it was during the Final Solution. Hitler was losing the war, but he was not going to lose the war against the Jews. So, because the crematoria could not take such an increase in numbers, pits were dug to cope with the transports of Hungarian Jews which by then were arriving two or three times a day.

I remember that a Gypsy camp nearby was emptied out and, soon after, a large group of midgets with their families were brought in. We were so jealous because their families had been allowed to stay together. Then, during one long, long night, they took them all away to be gassed, but because the crematoria were so overloaded they brought the bodies back and laid them in front of their barracks, like logs; It was two or three days before the bodies were hauled away and disposed of.

Auschwitz-Birkenau was created by liquidating a village next to Oswiecim. So of course the townspeople had to know what was going on. They saw two or three packed trains coming in through Cracow every day and then the same trains leaving, empty; they smelled the burning flesh – impossible that they did not know what was happening, but all the time I was in Birkenau no one came to the fence, no one offered to help us or tried to sneak any food to us – these people who went to church every Sunday. And the guards who worked in Auschwitz, I always wondered, when they went home at night, did they tell their children bedtime stories or did they tell them that they were shoving Jewish children into ovens?

We saw a group of about twenty men coming through the camp. As they were marching by, I watched – maybe I would know somebody. Suddenly, I saw my father. My first thought was to hide. It was terribly painful seeing him with his shaved head and in this uniform, like a prisoner. I couldn't imagine how he would feel if he

saw me also with a shaved head and in a rag. So I just wanted to hide. At that moment our eyes locked, and I could see tears rolling down his cheeks. That was the last time I saw my father.

After about six months, when some of us were selected by Mengele and

Greeting a resident of Užhorod, Renée revisits the pool where she used to swim fifty years ago

Renée with the archivist and a translator at Auschwitz.

Archives in Auschwitz recorded the entry of every prisoner. Note the listing of Renée's sister, Klara Weinfeld (pictured).

tables with huge books and we presumed they were going to put our name in it and give us a number. Then we realised that they were putting this number into our flesh – into our arms. I believe that the whole philosophy behind this tattooing was based on the fact that the Jewish religion does not permit tattoos – something the Nazis obviously knew about. So our numbers were entered into these huge books, but not our names because every woman was entered as Sara or Dora – a representation of a Jew, not a real human being; and if you are told often enough that you are not a human being – if you are treated as vermin – then you begin to believe it.

Even if somebody would have told us, we couldn't have accepted that it was possible for a group of people to be herded together and taken to a place for the purpose of being killed. How can a human being comprehend that? We heard of people being put into prison at the time of a war, but there was no precedence in the history of mankind when such a plan was devised with such premeditation and precision. There was just no precedence for that. So how should we have known that it was possible?

The Jews were the only people that were singled out and destroyed by fire – and that is why the word 'Holocaust' – a Greek

transferred to the barracks vacated by the midgets, Klara and I were separated. But we managed to meet at daybreak when it was still dark, just to tell each other that we were all right. On the eve of *Yom Kippur* there were all kinds of rumours because the Nazis always did something crazy on Friday nights or on Jewish holidays, so I was worried about Klara. The following morning she did not come to the wire separating the two camps – nor the next day – we heard that on *Yom Kippur* there had been a selection and that Klara had been selected out and she never returned.

There is an archive in Auschwitz that records the names of persons shipped out or murdered there. We were told when we arrived there that we were going to get a prisoner's number. They set up these

200	Brandstein		
	⁰/₀		
630	Roth · Zelma	1916	0
31	Schönfeld · Klári	1918	0
32	Wiesner – Cecília	1937	0
33	Kahan – Hanka	1921	0
34	Erös – Erzsébet	1898	0
35	Weinnau · Hedi	1922	0
36	Geisler · Iwesa	1916	0
37	Weinfeld · Klára	1928	0
38	Braun – Margit	1920	0
39	Singer · Elka	1915	0
640	Braun – Mopxa	1927	0
41	Bruchstein · Hajul	1913	0
42	Farkas · Katalin	1903	0

Inmates during a death march towards Wolfrathshausen, Germany, April 1945.

word meaning 'to burn' – applies only to the Jewish victims. Although several million non-Jewish people were also killed, no other race or nation was singled out for total destruction. Gypsies and midgets were collected wherever they were found, but for the Jews there was an actual plan to wipe out the entire race – everywhere in the world – that was the plan.

I can't explain how, but somehow I always knew I was going to survive; I felt doomed yet I couldn't imagine myself dying. In the last days of the War we were marched out of the camp to Krakow where we were herded into freezing cattle cars for a three-day journey to Mikolow where we were set to work in a factory and from where I was finally liberated. That was one of the miracles of my life because I had started that journey very sick with a high temperature but arrived cured! Another miracle was that my father had survived. He had collapsed on a death march to Theresenstadt and was found by the Soviets who took him to the hospital. But he died a few months after liberation. Finding my brother Frank, and Bernard – my husband of fifty-three years now – were two more miracles. But knowing that my mother and sister had perished made our survival and liberation very painful and bittersweet.

Hungarian Jewish women with their heads shaved are led into Auschwitz-Birkenau, June 1944.

Roll call in the women's camp of Auschwitz-Birkenau, 1944.

Hungarian Jewish women before and after processing in Auschwitz-Birkenau, 1944.

The overcrowded conditions of a
camp barrack in Auschwitz,
above which a banner states
'foster comradeship'.

Female prisoners in camp barracks
at the Auschwitz camp after
liberation by Soviet forces,
27 January 1945.

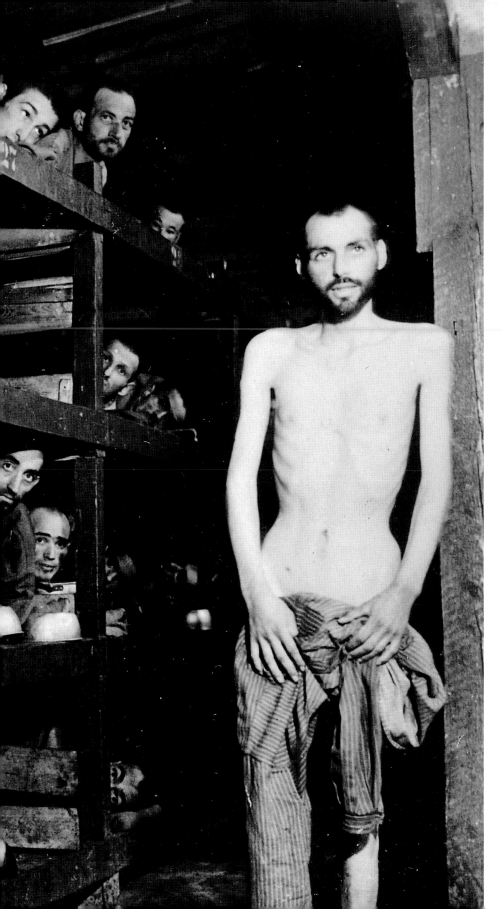

Prisoners in a barrack in the Buchenwald concentration camp.
The renowned writer Elie Wiesel is in the 2nd row from the bottom, 7th from left.

Inside Block 10, where experiments were conducted at Auschwitz.

Reichsführer SS Heinrich Himmler (fifth from left) reviews plans with officers at Auschwitz, 1942.

*Male prisoners assembled for roll
call at Buchenwald.*

*A prisoner who was unwilling or
unable to endure conditions in a
concentration camp committed
suicide by running into
electrified wire. The choice of
death by electrocution was often
only yards away.*

DARIO GABBAI

Dario Gabbai as he gives testimony to the Shoah Foundation.

SONDERKOMMANDO: SPECIAL COMMANDO. IN AUSCHWITZ-BIRKENAU AND OTHER DEATH CAMPS, THE *SONDERKOMMANDO* WAS A SPECIAL UNIT COMPOSED OF INMATES WHOSE PRIMARY FUNCTION WAS TO TRANSFER THE BODIES OF THOSE KILLED IN THE GAS CHAMBERS AND OTHER PARTS OF THE DEATH CAMPS TO THE CREMATORIA AND HANDLE THE BURNING OF THE BODIES. BEFORE CREMATION ITSELF, THEY WERE ALSO IN CHARGE OF REMOVING ALL ITEMS OF VALUE TO THE NAZI STATE (E.G. GLASSES, GOLD TEETH) FROM THE CORPSES AND THEIR ASHES. THE SS PERIODICALLY KILLED THE MEMBERS OF THE SPECIAL COMMANDO TO ENSURE THAT NO EYEWITNESSES TO THE MOST GRUESOME PART OF THEIR EXTERMINATION PROGRAM SURVIVED.

As far as I know there are only four of us who worked in the *Sonderkommando* who are still alive today. We were the only eyewitnesses that saw how 'the Final Solution' was done – the whole thing, from A to Z. I'm Jewish, from Greece and I lived in Greece until the time they took me to the concentration camp. It was the first week of April 1944 when I arrived in Auschwitz.

They selected some of the Greeks to work in block 13, in the *Sonderkommando* squad which was at the crematorium. On my first day there I couldn't understand what was going on; I saw 2,500 people, all naked, going into a big chamber. The gas chambers were built to fit 500 people but during this time the SS were putting in 2,500 people at a time. Nobody could do anything there but stand up, the children too, and fifteen minutes later, after they closed the chambers and the SS had thrown the gas into four openings, they opened the doors. And I saw the people I had seen fifteen minutes earlier – I saw them all dead, standing up with their children, all black and blue. I just couldn't work out what was

*A line of ovens in a crematorium of
Auschwitz-Birkenau, 1943.*

going on. There was a Polish guy there and I asked him 'Where is God?' and he replied 'God is where you have your strength.'

There were four crematoria and every crematorium had eight or nine ovens working 24 hours a day. My instructions were to put the women on the outside of the oven and the men inside so that the fat on the women, who had more than the men, could burn more easily. We then had to pulverise the ashes and take them to the river which was not too far away.

One time I had two friends, very close friends of mine, who came in. I told them right away that they were going to die. They asked for food and I gave them whatever I had. I told them where exactly to place themselves, near the openings, so they could die quickly; it took two to four minutes, depending on where you were standing. And after they were through, I took them out, washed them and put them in the oven to be burned. It was terrible; the only thing you could see after they opened up the gas chambers was a lot of blood because the people were scratching the walls, trying to get out. But there was no escape, no place to go, and no-one survived. There were a lot of big shots from Berlin coming to watch the gassing. You know, there was a hermetically closed hole in the gas chamber and they were looking in there to see how the Jewish people were

dying. But if there were only thirty or forty people that were not sent to the gas chambers; we had to hold them up by their ears and the SS would shoot them in the back. Afterwards we had to pull them around and clean the blood off them.

A lot of people think that those of us working in the *Sonderkommando* were guilty of something because we were doing this kind of work. But we couldn't get out of it. If we didn't do whatever they asked, they would have killed us right away.

When the Red Army was approaching, the Germans marched us to Austria; of the thousands who were on the march, only a few hundred survived, including ninety-six *Sonderkommando*. There was one good morning when we woke up to an unexpected silence – all the Germans had gone and the Americans came a few hours later. That was on May 6, 1945 – and I weighed just sixty-seven pounds.

It was difficult for many, many years. The first ten years after I came out of the camp I had nightmares practically every single night. It still affects me because I'm not in a position to do certain things I would like to do; I don't have the ability to do things as a result of a psychological thing inherited from the concentration camp. For years I was silent and kept all this to myself – just trying to keep alive – but now I want to tell my story to the world.

DISPOSAL OF THE BODIES

Corpses being dragged by Sonderkommando (see page 157) to fire pits for disposal at Auschwitz-Birkenau, summer 1944. When the ovens in the crematoria were insufficient to process the many corpses, the bodies were burned in ditches.

An incinerating oven at
Bergen-Belsen

Sonderkommando *at work in one*
of the crematoria at Auschwitz.

Auschwitz guards with containers of Zyklon-B gas for the camp gas chambers.

A copy of architectural plans for Crematoria II and III, dated 27 January 1942.

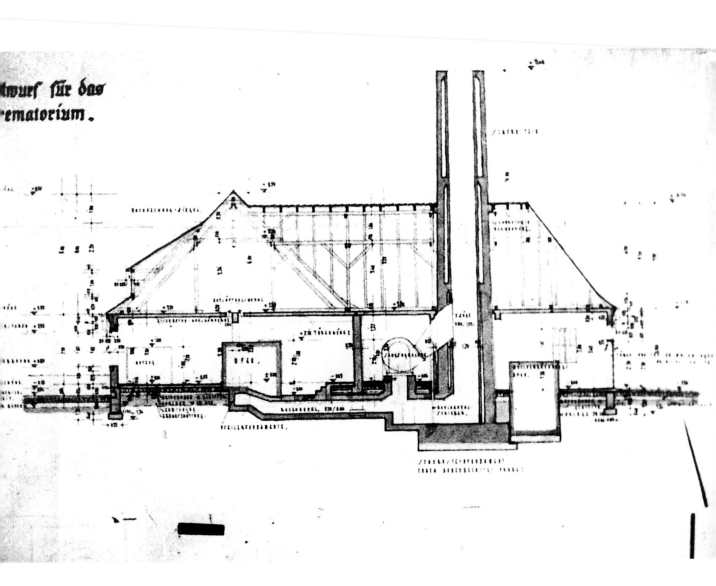

*One of the five crematoria of the
Auschwitz-Birkenau death camp*

The wedding rings taken from Buchenwald camp prisoners, discovered after the liberation on 11 April 1945.

Prisoners finish work inside Crematorium II, Auschwitz-Birkenau, 1943.

TOM LANTOS

Budapest was a magnificent, world-class European city. Beginning in the middle of the nineteenth century – when Jews got full civil, political and religious rights – there was an incredible symbiotic relationship between Hungarians and Jews. The population of Hungary in its boundaries at the time was only about 45 per cent Hungarian. The rest of the people were Slovaks, Romanians, Croats, Serbs, Germans, and others. In order to have a Hungarian majority within the boundaries of Hungary, the government declared that Jews were Hungarians of the Israelite faith. And when Jews were counted with Catholic and Protestant Hungarians, there was a Hungarian majority.

This was an extremely important thing until the First World War. At the end of the war, almost two-thirds of the territory of Hungary was taken away. What was left was overwhelmingly Hungarian with virtually no ethnic minorities. It was no longer important for Jews to be considered Hungarian; Jews were again considered Jews. The first antisemitic laws in twentieth-century Europe were not in Germany, Austria or Poland, but in Hungary. In 1923 the Hungarian parliament passed a law which restricted the number of Jews who could enter university to the proportion of Jews in the Hungarian population.

When you speak of Jews in Hungary, you are really talking about two entirely different groups. There were the assimilated Jews of Budapest and the other larger cities, and there were the very religious Jews in north-eastern and eastern Hungary. The bulk of the Jews in Budapest were utterly assimilated. Many of them, like my family, were deeply patriotic, and included military officers, university professors, writers, and they were

Tom Lantos and Annette Tillemann, the person he later married, both as young children in Budapest, Hungary.

MÁS 8 OLDALAS KÉPES MELLÉKLET　Vasárnapi szám ÁRA 10 FILLÉR

Függetlenség

POLITIKAI NAPILAP

HITLER AUSZTRIÁBAN

Első útja szülővárosába, Braunauba vezetett Linzben tomboló lelkesedéssel fogadták – A vezér és kancellár vasárnap vonul be Bécsbe

Történelmi kiáltvány a német nemzethez

Hitler útban Bécs felé

'Hitler in Austria' Függetlenség *(Independence) Newspaper, 13 March 1938.*

enormously proud of their Hungarian cultural heritage.

I was born in Budapest in 1928. Hitler came to power five years later, in 1933. As a child, I remember that family conversation focused overwhelmingly on what would happen to us. In 1938, when I was ten years old, I bought my first newspaper. I was walking home from school, and I saw the headlines, 'Hitler marches into Austria'. I sensed that this moment, this event would have a tremendous impact on the lives of Hungarian Jews, my family and myself.

I was very much aware of antisemitism. Jewish boys walking to and from school were often attacked. There was a Hungarian Nazi movement with its own emblem, which was the arrow cross. This became the most hated and feared symbol throughout the war. It was worse for Hungarian Jews than the swastika, because the Hungarian Nazis – to prove that they were more Nazi, more loyal to Hitler, than Germans – outdid them in cruelty and viciousness.

When Hitler invaded the Soviet Union in the summer of 1941, he needed additional troops. He demanded that both Hungary and Romania provide large numbers of army divisions to fight alongside the Germans on the Soviet front. Both countries were vying for Hitler's favour, because Hitler had divided Transylvania between Hungary and Romania in 1940. (The area had been Hungarian before 1918 and Romania had taken all of it after the First World War.) When Hitler demanded troops, both countries eagerly responded in the hopes of getting additional territory in the Carpathian basin. When Hungarian troops went to the eastern front, this was the first time that Hungarian Jews were forbidden to serve in the army and were instead taken to the Soviet front to do the dirty work: they dug the trenches, they carried the ammunition, they walked through minefields to clear the way for the troops. Most of the young Jewish men who left for the Soviet front never returned. Every single young man in my extended family, my cousins and a young uncle, all went to the Soviet front and all perished. We do not know whether they froze to death, whether they contracted some disease, whether they starved to death or whether they were killed.

My Christian classmates reacted to Hitler's invasion in different ways. Some remained good friends. Some made me feel that they continued to be my friends, but they didn't want to be seen in public with me, particularly not after we had to wear the yellow Star of David, which was one of the Hungarian government's edicts after Hitler came into the country. Some turned against Jews in general and me in particular.

On the one hand I was still in love with Hungarian literature and music and history, and I continued studying it through early 1944. At the same time the seamy side, the dark side of the Hungarian national character was becoming more and more obvious. Jews were losing their jobs, their businesses, they didn't have the right to practise their professions and they were physically persecuted.

While a handful of Hungarian Christians were helpful, a vast number were bystanders – some with regret and sorrow, some with very different feelings. There was a very sizeable group that loved the persecution of the Jews. Persecuting Jews not only satisfied their deeply ingrained antisemitism, it also gave them an opportunity to take the homes and jobs and property of the Jews. Most people did not participate actively, but they allowed it to happen. There was no feeling that the non-Jewish population was with you. You had the feeling that they were against you, or they were looking away. There was a tremendous amount of confusion in my mind as a fourteen-, fifteen-, sixteen-year-old.

Of course there was the on-going debate within my family and within all families as to whether we should try to leave, or whether we should hope that although things were bad, we would survive. The discussions were interminable: did we have a chance in Hungary, or should we make an attempt to leave? But this was our home – people had their professions, had elderly parents; their whole world was Budapest. While in 1938 the intelligent ones could have left, by 1944 – when Nazi Germany occupied Hungary – no one could leave.

The range of knowledge about what was happening ran the gamut from those who knew practically nothing to those who followed the unfolding of the war in

Tom and Annette as they give testimony to the Shoah Foundation.

considerable detail. The difference between the least well informed and the best informed was the ability to listen to the BBC. The BBC was our lifeline to the outside world. Every evening we would close the shutters, lower the curtains and huddle around the radio set. When the reception was good, an electronic eye in the set would come together; when the reception was not quite as good, the eye was incomplete. So we would tune the radio by watching the eye. We hung on to the BBC every night. We had maps and we charted the course of all the campaigns, literally kilometre by kilometre. We knew what was happening. We knew about the battle of Stalingrad, that it represented a turning point when the Nazis were pushed back. We were convinced that the Germans were losing the war, and that it was just a question of time before they would have to capitulate.

When Hitler occupied Hungary on 19 March 1944, I was sixteen years old. I joined the Hungarian Underground. It was basically a number of not very well organised groups, small clusters of individuals. A handful of these people were engaged in military activities. But increasingly these people organised under Raoul Wallenberg's leadership, to provide food, medical supplies and a feeling of being a protected community which hopefully would survive the war under Swedish, Swiss, Spanish or Vatican protection. As 1944 wore on, I really didn't think I had much of a chance of surviving the Second World War. I felt that I was trapped in Hungary, surrounded by the Nazis. Although the Soviets were coming, I thought we would be done for before they arrived. Of course that was Eichmann's plan, that was Hitler's plan. It was Raoul Wallenberg who interposed his frail body between the Nazi war machine and thousands and thousands of Jewish men, women and children. Had it not been for him, neither I nor the other tens of thousands of others would have survived to January 1945.

Raoul Wallenberg is the central figure in my life. He was the son of Sweden's most distinguished family. In the summer of 1944, at the behest of the American government, he accepted an assignment to come to Budapest, to join the Swedish embassy there, for the sole purpose of trying to save Jewish lives. At the risk of his own life he saved them. He saved lives by issuing so-called Swedish protected passports, which were pieces of paper with an embassy seal. These documents declared that the individual who possessed this document planned to go to Sweden as an immigrant at the end of the war, and therefore, effective immediately, he or she was under the protection of the Royal Swedish Government. Well, this was like me declaring you to be a prima ballerina of the St Petersburg Ballet – it had no validity. But in the chaos and confusion of the war, and with Wallenberg threatening the Nazis that unless they honoured these worthless pieces of paper they would be punished as war criminals, these miraculous, worthless pieces of paper worked.

They worked not only for the people who got them from Wallenberg, but they

Jewish labour battalions were utilised to build and repair important communication links and bridges and to dig trenches on the Eastern Front.

also inspired the Swiss government, the Portuguese government, the Spanish government and the Vatican to do the same thing. For instance, my wife Annette was saved by Portuguese papers that were an outgrowth of Wallenberg's work.

The phrase 'no good deed goes unpunished' has never been truer than in the case of Wallenberg. He left behind the comfort, the safety, the security of neutral Sweden and went down into the hell that was Budapest in 1944. In the countryside the Jews had already been put into cattle cars and shipped to Auschwitz. What was left was the extermination of the Jewish population of Budapest. Not quite single-handedly, but under his leadership, a handful of people saved tens of thousands of individuals who survived the determination of the Nazis to kill them, as

they did the Jews of the countryside. And they did not. They could not, because of Wallenberg's courage. There is no doubt in my mind that Wallenberg was the ultimate humanitarian hero of the Second World War. Had there been just a few hundred Raoul Wallenbergs, with the courage of his convictions, with the recognition that we are all our brothers' and sisters' keepers, then this brutal nightmare might have been averted. Here was a man who did not share with us his nationality, his language or his religion – he was a Lutheran. What we shared was our common humanity. He felt that we were his brothers and sisters. And he decided to risk his life – and ultimately he gave his life, he spent the remainder of his life in Soviet prisons – to save his fellow human beings. There is nothing that any university could teach our children that is as important as Raoul Wallenberg's lesson, that we are all our brothers' keepers.

My greatest asset was that I looked very Aryan – tall, blue-eyed and blond. The only danger I faced was that if German or Hungarian soldiers became suspicious of me or others, they would do their best to make us take down our pants, because only Jews were circumcized. I had friends who had to drop their pants and were shot on the spot. You never knew whom you could trust. You were in a jungle surrounded by jungle animals. Some would merely wish you ill, while some would actively go after you. The first step of resistance was not to wear the yellow Star of David. The penalty if you were caught could be anything. If the soldier you encountered was a monster, he could whip out his revolver and shoot you dead on the spot. Many people were killed that way. If a soldier was less vicious, he could throw you in prison, or beat you up.

Tom returns with his four of his 17 grandchildren to the bridge in northern Hungary where he was forced to work in a labour battalion during the German occupation of Hungary.

Jews gathered on the platform of the Jozsefváros station in Budapest, Hungary, autumn 1944. Raoul Wallenberg stands on the right with his hands clasped. He appears to be negotiating for the freedom and life of Jews being deported to concentration camps.

I was caught and put into a forced labour camp. I was taken with a group of men to an important railroad bridge north of Budapest. Our job was to repair the bridge, which the British and American bombers were continually damaging. It was an important communication link for the German military. The Allies knew it was important and they did a very good job of bombing it. On the one hand, we hated to see the bridge bombed, because that meant we had to repair it. On the other hand, we hoped they would be successful because they were our only hope of liberation.

I escaped from that labour camp, but I was captured and beaten to a pulp. After a second escape I gradually made my way to Budapest and Wallenberg. I became one of the hundreds of unimportant little people, a small cog in the Wallenberg machine, which saved many thousands of Hungarian Jewish lives.

When I was sent to forced labour, initially my parents were in Budapest. Then my mother was deported, and later on my father as well. I have no idea what happened to my mother. My father survived the war. It was obvious to me as it was to all of us that families as units would not survive. It was clear that if we were to survive, we would survive each of us on our own. The Germans would not allow family units to function as family units. The

thought of a sixteen-year-old boy leaving his parents was not part of my thinking. There was nothing I could do for my parents and there was nothing they could do for me. I was not young any more. I was very old. I was sixteen, but I was very old. The bloodbath, the cruelty, the death that I saw, so many times around me during those few months between March of 1944 and January of 1945 made me a very old young man.

Wallenberg leased large apartment houses, most of them along the banks of the Danube, where he put up signs indicating that all the residents in these houses were under the protection of the Royal Swedish Government. I stayed in a Wallenberg-protected house at St Stephen Park, number 25, on the second floor. The street was named after St Stephen, Hungary's first king, and the park and the houses still stand today. Most of these were upper middle class apartment houses. The ones that surrounded St Stephen Park were very pleasant. These were three-bedroom apartments, which may have had four, five or six people living there before the war. Suddenly they became hovels with fifty, sixty or seventy people jammed into each apartment.

In the apartment where I lived was a man suffering from asthma. One of my jobs in the underground was to go out into

The war-ravaged streets of Budapest, 1945.

the city without my yellow star and find pharmacies to get medicine for this man. Passing as a Hungarian Christian, I delivered messages, picked up food and found medical supplies. I roamed through Budapest and could do so because of my Aryan looks. There were very few of us who could pass as Christians, but I was one of them.

The word 'protected' was a misnomer, because many of the people living in these 'protected' houses could be taken any day. There was one occasion when the people in the protected house next to the one I was living in were ordered by a group of Nazi military or police – Hungarian or German –

down to the Danube. They were machine-gunned or shot one by one and their bodies pushed into the river. It was as simple as that. The 'protected' house only provided protection when the good Lord and good fortune were with you.

Budapest was a large city – two million people. And while there were Jewish districts, Jews lived throughout the city. In Budapest the Germans could not begin the kind of mass deportation that they could do in a town of 15,000 people, where everybody knew who was Jewish. There had to be a mechanism to push all the Jews into defined areas. They did it by creating two ghettos – one in the heart of the city around the main synagogue, and an international ghetto along the Danube, which basically consisted of Wallenberg's protected houses and protected houses of other embassies. As the war unfolded and as these preparations were taking place, the opportunity for mass deportations by trains became more and more difficult. The Germans were in an increasingly desperate military situation. The availability of cattle cars was diminishing. Towards the end, there was a mass march towards the Austrian border, with largely Hungarian Nazis and their dogs driving mobs of people, mainly old and very young, mainly women. Many perished along the way. Many more perished once they reached their destination. Wallenberg played a heroic role by pulling people out of the forced march by going to the Austro-Hungarian border and picking out large numbers of people and claiming they were Swedish citizens. These were the last chaotic weeks and days of the Second World War in Hungary. The sadism, the cruelty, the irrationality of the German and Hungarian Nazis was unbelievable.

We knew of the approach of the Red Army through the BBC and the sound of the artillery. We could hear the artillery moving closer and closer. Then one night, at about one o'clock in the morning there was a great commotion in our building and a group of Soviet soldiers broke in. There were two or three people in the building who spoke some Russian. They told the soldiers who we were and, fortunately, the commanding officer, a very intelligent and educated fellow, understood the situation. He posted some of his people around the building for protection. When we went to bed, we were under Nazi control but when dawn came we had been liberated by the Soviet army. It was an almost indescribable feeling to be under the protective umbrella of the anti-Nazi Allies. And while we knew there were still many hardships ahead, we knew that our lives were safe. It was total euphoria. It was like having to undergo an operation where the chances of losing your life are 99.9 per cent – and you survive. The closer we came to liberation, the more I was convinced that I would not survive. This was realism. But despite the odds, I made it.

Of course, at that moment we could focus on who else had survived: did your mother survive? Did your best friend? Did your girlfriend? One of the most painful things was that I did not know for months whether my mother or other members of my family would ever return. It was only in the summer of 1945 that the awful realisation set in that my mother would never return. There were, however, more

horrendous stories than mine. I know of a young woman, whose husband survived Auschwitz and returned to Budapest. On his way to rejoin his wife, he was picked up by Soviet troops and sent to Siberia. He returned several years later only to find his wife had married and had a child. These are the routine stories of Jews in Hungary in the Second World War.

After the Soviet troops occupied Budapest, those of us who lived there were subjected to the Russian Liberation Forces. Their antics ranged all the way from large Russian women trying to rape young Hungarian boys, to people being rounded up and shipped off to Siberia, not to reappear for years. But the standard looting was, compared to the Holocaust, mere irritations. I mean, in the midst of all the misbehaviour of the Soviet troops, and there was a great deal of that, including very ugly incidents, it was still a liberation.

I was on the university campus one day soon after the war, and I saw an announcement that a US scholarship might be available for people who spoke English. I applied, although I never dreamed I would be selected. I was on cloud nine when I was. I left Budapest on a crowded train on 8 August 1947, via Vienna and Paris. I had a ticket on a converted troopship, the SS *Marine Falcon*. I went down to the harbour and found my

ship. I went to my bunk and they called for chow. I had no idea what chow was, it was not part of my English vocabulary. But I got into the chow line – and this was a period when of course I was still totally preoccupied with food, I had spent protracted periods, years, with very little food. I was dreaming about food, it was the beginning and end of my goals and objectives. And these wonderful people slopped all these wonderful things on this big metal tray. At the end of the line there was a huge wicker basket of oranges, and a huge wicker basket of bananas. My mother had always taught me to do the right thing, and I did not know what the right thing was, so I asked this enormous sailor, 'Sir, do I take a banana, or do I take an orange?' And he said, 'Man, you can eat all the damn bananas and all the damn oranges you want.' And then I knew I was in heaven. And I loaded up on bananas and oranges, and I got very sick, but I loved every minute of it.

Both my parents were deeply pro-America, and they knew a great deal about the United States from reading, although neither had ever been there. I had also read a lot. So in an academic sense I had an understanding of the place. But when the SS *Marine Falcon* pulled into New York harbour, and I saw this incredible skyline, and the vast wealth of this gigantic city, I

The converted US navy vessel SS Marine Falcon, which transported Tom Lantos to America.

The end of German occupation in Budapest, February 1945

*Tom and Annette Lantos with four
of their 17 grandchildren (left to
right) Corban Tilleman-Dick,
Kismet Swett, Chanteclaire Swett
and Liberty Tilleman-Dick at the
Dohany Street Synagogue,
Budapest, Hungary.*

felt like a very naive child from a village. I got a second-class train ticket from New York to Seattle. To the University of Washington. I threw myself into academic life, but there were all kinds of old people dependent on me financially, so within weeks I had a bunch of part-time jobs, ranging from stacking grocery shelves at night to ushering at the Seattle Symphony in a borrowed tuxedo.

My life today, given my background, is something I cannot believe possible. At the end of my life I am privileged to serve the Congress of the United States. I think back to my life fifty years ago, when I was a hunted animal in the jungle, and now I am dealing with issues of state of a country I love so deeply. It all seems like a dream and it all places an incredible sense of responsibility on me. I didn't achieve this because of what I am, it happened because of what this country is.

My wife Annette and I have known each other all of our lives. We grew up together as children in Budapest, and we have been married now for forty-nine years. And if the next forty-nine years are half as good as the first forty-nine, I'll be a very lucky man. We have two daughters who very early on came to us and said that they planned a special gift for us. As our families had been wiped out in the Holocaust, they would give us a large family. And we have been blessed with seventeen wonderful grandchildren.

There were three reasons why people like me survived. The first and overwhelming reason was the presence and heroism of Raoul Wallenberg. Without him, none of us would have survived. Secondly, it was perhaps our skill, our physical stamina. And finally it was pure luck. Had I run into a Nazi patrol, had they ordered me to drop my pants, I would have been killed on the spot. I suspect that of these three elements, Wallenberg and luck were the overriding factors.

The Soviet red flag is raised over Budapest, 1945.

A survivor delouses himself after liberation from Bergen-Belsen.

Liberated survivors stare from behind the fence, Bergen-Belsen, January 1945.

A surviving French prisoner from the Dora-Nordhausen concentration camp after liberation by the 1st US Army in 1945.

A Hungarian Jew, one of the few prisoners within Bergen-Belsen still able to walk.

Surviving prisoners stand by the Auschwitz camp fence.

*Documents of a former prisoner
of the Dachau concentration
camp, which were submitted as
evidence to the Central
Commission for the
Investigation of Nazi Crimes.*

Documentation discovered on the site of Auschwitz detailing the mass extermination of Jews.
The document was written in Hebrew by an unidentified camp prisoner assigned to the crematorium squad.

Soviet soldiers from Stalingrad
stream through the streets of
Budapest.

*Street fighting continues in
Budapest as Soviet forces advance,
January 1945.*

*Hungarian soldiers search for
German mines and booby traps in
the abandoned houses of Budapest,
February 1945.*

Wooden crosses in a bombed
cemetery in Budapest.

The inmates of Dachau concentration camp celebrate the liberation of the camp by American forces. Established in March 1933, Dachau endured throughout the twelve years of the Third Reich.

The release of prisoners from the Auschwitz concentration camp

*The horrific scene of mass
annihilation within the
Nordhausen concentration camp*

*The camp doctor of Bergen-Belsen,
Doctor Fritz Klein was responsible
for many experiments on camp
prisoners. British soldiers arrest
him after the liberation of Bergen-
Belsen, April 1945.*

A trainload of slave workers
from concentration camps were
beaten to death and buried in
shallow graves in woodland.
German civilians are forced to
exhume the bodies and bury them
in new graves.

Female prisoners drag away a corpse, helping to clear away the atrocities of Bergen-Belsen.

SS prisoners load corpses onto trucks for burial, Bergen-Belsen.

Surviving prisoners sit among the dead, Bergen-Belsen, 1945.

*Liberated prisoners use the
stock pile of shoes as fuel.*

Emaciated survivors of one of the largest Nazi concentration camps at Ebensee, Austria. The camp was entered on 7 May 1945 by the 80th division, US Third Army.

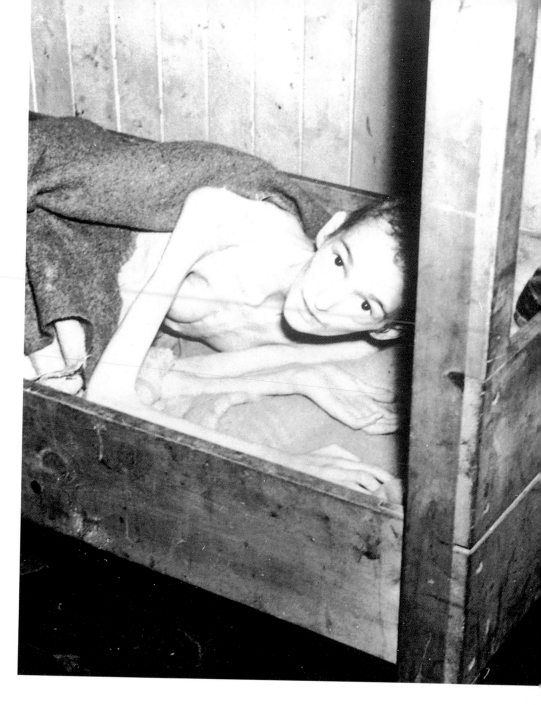

*Surviving prisoners of the
Buchenwald concentration camp.*

*An emaciated female prisoner
suffering from typhus in the Bergen-
Belsen camp hospital barrack.*

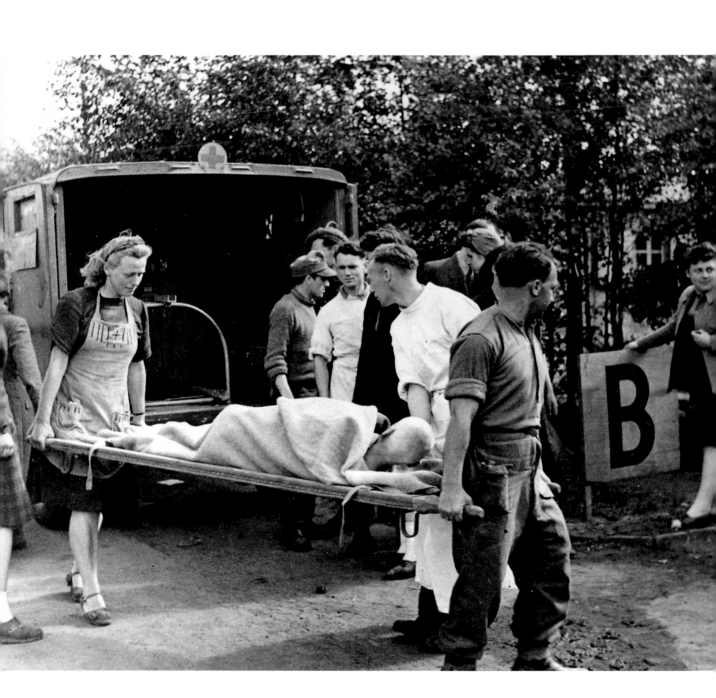

A typhus case is taken to a British military hospital assisted by German civilians.

Alice Lok Cahana (lying down) with other survivors preparing food just after being liberated at Bergen-Belsen.

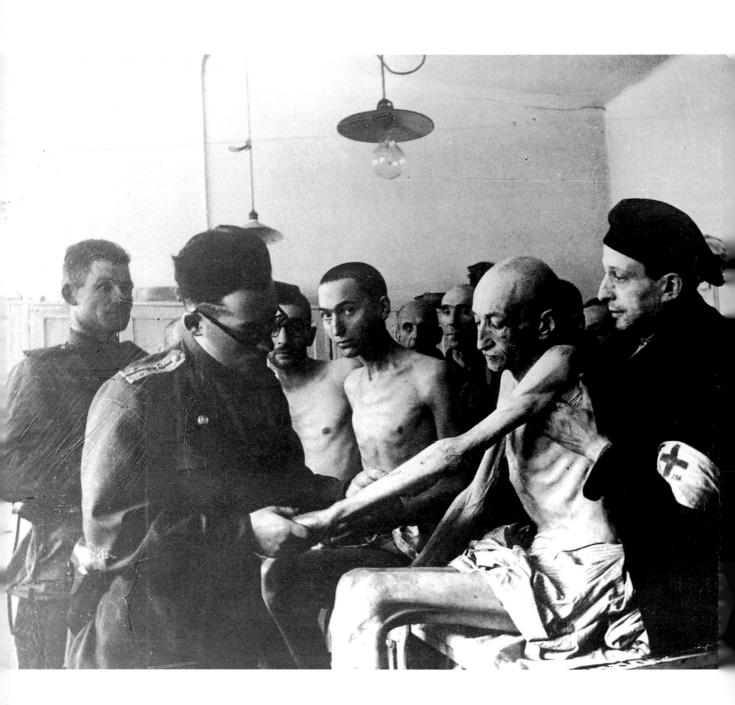

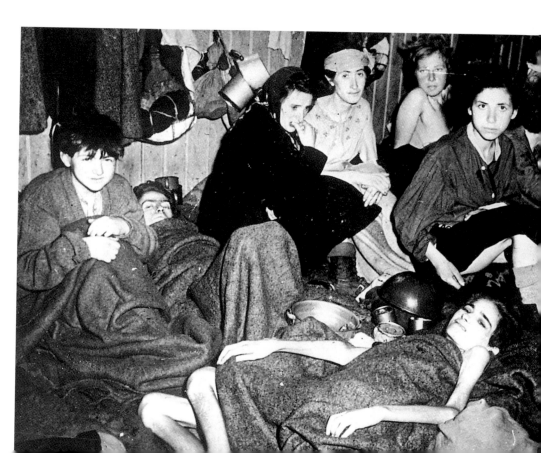

Opposite: A Soviet army doctor examining the prisoners at Auschwitz-Birkenau. January, 1945.

Members of the Red Cross carry a young boy out of Auschwitz-Birkenau extermination camp.

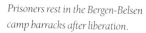

Prisoners rest in the Bergen-Belsen camp barracks after liberation.

Unwilling witnesses: German civilians are brought to see the atrocities of Buchenwald.

German civilians gaze at a pile of bones, the remains of approximately 400 Buchenwald prisoners.

A sign at the entrance to the site of the Bergen-Belsen concentration camp.

Jewish emigrants leave Germany
after World War II.

In cooperation with US
Immigration, HIAS organise a
special alien registration bureau
to assist the registration of
non-citizens. New York, 1952.

Opposite: The last resting place
of approximately 5,000
concentration camp victims,
Buchenwald.

THREE SOLDIERS' STORIES

DR PAUL PARKS

The city of Indianapolis, where I grew up was a self-contained black community: the police were black, the firemen were black, in our schools all the teachers and the principal were black. The only white people in my street were Vern and Gabe Seigel who had a little Jewish store. My father was a Seminole Indian, and my mother was half black and half Indian; they had been induced to come off the Reservation in Florida and move to Indiana to work in the foundries, where my father thought he could make a lot of money. He came to the town of Marion, thinking this would be the world of opportunity and suddenly realised that he was a labourer in a foundry. When he contracted tuberculosis we moved to Indianapolis where there was a sanatorium.

My earliest memory of discrimination was because my family was different; although my mother soon became acculturated, my father wore different clothing and retained his beliefs in a world where he would be able to hunt and fish to support his family. The only other people who were also different, because of their ethnic background, were Daniel and his family. Daniel and I became very close, because we were constantly fighting off these black kids who called us names and attacked us. My mother would explain that we must take pride in our difference and she also told me I would never win by fighting everybody.

I left that community only when I went to Purdue University and here it was very different, because there were only seven of us who were black. I'd never been in a classroom with whites; it was an altogether new setting. Because we were black, we couldn't stay in the dormitories, we couldn't eat in certain sections of the union building and we were forbidden – on pain of expulsion – to date a white female. The university kept telling us that we ought to go to the School of Agriculture because there'd always be a place for small-time farmers, but there was no place for us in engineering because the university took pride in the fact that they found jobs for anybody who graduated. There was no way, they told us, they could do the same for us because there just wasn't anybody who was going to hire black engineers. I was determined to stay and told the Dean so, but I was constantly afraid that I would get into some trouble – that's the sort of uncomfortable environment we were in.

This was in 1941. The reason I went into the army the following summer was because a law had been passed to draft 18-year-olds. I was just eighteen, but if you had decent averages, the university would give you a deferment until you finished college education. I figured I got decent averages and would be exempted. Then I got a letter from the draft board, which, on the advice of a friend, I ignored. Soon after, this fellow came to my door and told me that I had 48 hours to present myself at the draft board. I appealed to the university and was given a sealed letter – the last time I ever took a letter about me without reading it first. I took it to the draft board and it said, 'We recommend this young man be drafted immediately.' When I asked why, the Dean told me it was because I caused problems.

When I see people who were survivors of the Holocaust, I reflect on the differences between what happened to the Jews in Germany and black slavery: the black folk brought here started out as slaves and were never a free people in this country until the Civil War. You need to explain to people who question why the Jews allowed the Holocaust to happen to them. They lived in a country among people they thought of as friends and neighbours and Germany was a country which they had learned to trust. They were part of it, they had helped it to grow, they had helped build it and they had prospered and lived freely in it. It was very hard for them, I'm sure, to believe that their country would herd them together and do something so terrible to them. They thought that when the Germans began keeping lists of all Jews, this was a pretty normal procedure – not in order to kill them. I guess it was like here in the United States when they wanted to assess who's black and who's white and who's something else; ordinarily they understood that the census information was going to be used positively. We never think about the United States using that census in a negative way – in order to destroy us.

The Holocaust was a form of slavery – some of the Jews they enslaved were forced to work and to do things because they had certain skills. So there are similarities

Dr Paul Parks with the menorah he was given by a Dachau survivor he liberated. The survivor managed to make the menorah while still a prisoner.

between slavery and the Holocaust. There were people in the United States who brought in Africans from certain kinds of tribal groups who were violent and vicious and fought back. They killed all those people; they got rid of them because they were threatening the whole thing. I think that at the core of all of this is a decision on the part of a group of people that they're better, that they're more important than someone else and that on some scale of their own devising they are at the top and everybody else is at the very bottom. In the same way, the Germans saw the Jews as a threat and thought they would take over the country so they decided to get rid of them; one form of slavery was supposedly to keep an economy from being destroyed, the other, the one using black slaves, was used to build up a major economy.

I meet Holocaust survivors, these same people whom I first saw in Dachau, and I'm just amazed to see how well they look. But at the same time, when you talk to them, tears run down their faces when they talk about family members who were killed and about everything they went through. One of my dear friends just keeps remembering

all the things that happened but he no longer cries in sadness, only in joy for the fact that he has had the opportunity to live the life he's had as an adult in America. I wish many more people could hear this man and understand that what we've got is so precious, so important, that it ought not to be destroyed by people making silly judgements about each other.

About our role near the end of the war, though I have no proof of this, a Bostonian who was on General Eisenhower's staff told me that the decision was taken that, wherever possible, the liberators of the camps would be black soldiers – United States soldiers. He said that they had come to the conclusion that if the people who were in the camps saw black soldiers they would feel more at ease with them. It wasn't some sort of weird, cruel trick – people who saw us come into the camps, some of them my friends now, have told me, 'We knew when we saw you that you weren't Germans … we knew you had to be Americans' – so it did work.

After the War, I went back to college – back to Purdue – and I went straight away to see the Dean and told him 'I'm back and I've registered at this University.' He told me that I could not do that and that I didn't have to finish. But he left the College, the dormitories were integrated and we were able to take advantage of all the amenities in the institution. Black students no longer have to feel uncomfortable – it's what I hoped for.

One day, some time in 1972 or '73, I remember it was on a Sunday, someone knocked at my door and when I opened it I saw this man holding something wrapped up in a newspaper. He said, 'Are you Paul Parks?' I said 'Yes.' He said, 'You know, we've been looking for you for several years. Off and on, people have been looking for you.' I said, 'Why?' He said, 'Well, there was this fellow who was liberated by you at Dachau who remembered you. And he made a menorah in the camp. He made it out of concrete nails and welded it together, brazed it together while he was in the camp. He kept this menorah all this time, and before he died, he told his family that he wanted you to have it. So we've been looking for you to give it to you. And here it is.' And this fellow gave me this beautiful menorah for having been one of the people who liberated Dachau. I've always loved it, maybe it's not perfect, but to me it's perfectly beautiful. It just makes me feel good, the idea that here is something so well done under conditions that had to be the worst in the world. I do have several decorations for being in the war, but I have never thought of myself as a hero – or a liberator of a camp; I was there by sheer accident – but it did happen. I guess that all of us who participated in the war in Europe made it possible to open up the camps. And I believe that the man who made this menorah wanted to acknowledge that, as a result of our participation, he was free and could walk among the rest of us with a sense of his own personal pride. The fact that he died before we had a chance to talk to each other about it leaves me a little sad, but I now have a piece of him here and I can sense a little of how he would have been feeling when he was making this.

I had left Germany with a very bitter taste against German people and, years later, I had a strange experience. My wife and I were at the Olympics in Barcelona and a friend of mine had arranged tickets for the events we wished to see. But what I didn't realise was that the seats were in the German section of the stadium. As I sat down beside this fellow – he was about my own age – he swung away from me as far as he could and said, 'I don't want the likes of you touching me' – in this guttural German accent. My wife asked me what I had said to that man, because he'd turned as white as a sheet, she thought it was out of fear, though I had done or said nothing in response. I wanted to say, 'Hey, wait a minute, we're past all that now,' but the thing that was so encouraging about that whole incident was that there was a group of young Germans sitting just below us and these kids turned to me and said, 'Mister, we want to apologise – he should not have said such a thing, nor should he even have felt such a thing,' and I thought then that maybe there is some hope – maybe.

That incident has made me hopeful that perhaps there are some changes going on – but I'm still not going to Germany; every time they talk about the German Army I get frightened – because of what I saw of the Germans when I was there – a country that was scientifically and mechanically brilliant but politically stupid. They looked at the differences between them and the rest of the world and felt that they were far superior.

After what I had experienced, I did not wish to bring kids into such a cruel world – I felt strongly about it. I love children, but I hate to think of bringing them into a world where they would be hated from the day they were born, simply on the basis of their skin colour. Who wants to live in this kind of a world and be treated this way – and how dare people make a decision about the value of my children. But I did have children and all of them went to college and have degrees, and now they have children of their own. But although they're doing well, periodically they still face people who make a judgement about them because of

the colour of their skin. So despite everything, all the courage and all the things that we've ever done, we have to face the fact that some people still make judgements based on colour or creed. I get very emotional on this subject, but I've learned to live with it. Now, maybe someone says you ought not to feel that way, but, as my daddy used to say: 'Walk in my shoes, and then see how well it feels'. That's why I was in the Civil Rights Movement, because I believe I have to give my children a world where they can live in peace and with people who respect them on the basis of what they are able to achieve. That's what my father taught me – that's what I have told the many children I have taught: people may have certain eyes, certain noses, whatever – you can't make judgements on these things – they are neither positive nor negative factors.

I'm an old man now, but as long as I'm able to stand upright I will fight against this disease, because that's what those people who were in Dachau were saying; that's the dream that those people who escaped have – that this nation, that the world, will not do this to anybody else again.

WARREN DUNN

Warren Dunn, a liberator of the Dachau concentration camp.

I was about fifteen when the war started in Europe and at that time I lived in Santa Barbara, California. We didn't really attach much significance to the war because it was far away, in a foreign country, and I was just concerned to enjoy life. We heard very little about what was happening to the Jews in Europe, I don't think there was any awareness of people being incarcerated in Germany, in Poland and other areas; until I was actually in the concentration camp I had absolutely no knowledge of people being gassed and cremated.

My first experience of this was in Dachau. As a company commander I was ordered to liberate the camp which I thought might contain several hundred POWs. We arrived at six o'clock in the morning with instructions to talk to the prisoners and to assure them that help was coming from medical and food service personnel. But before we got there another unit had captured some of the guards, and many of the Germans who were not able to flee, and they had actually executed them – stood them up against the wall and shot them. In fact the company commander was court-marshalled because of that but you know, when you see this kind of thing and the people responsible, it gives rise to a tremendous amount of hate.

The first thing we saw outside the camp on railroad tracks was forty boxcars – I believe that was the count – absolutely filled with dead bodies. Then we shot the locks off the gate and went inside and saw thousands more bodies lying around the whole compound. And not having had any knowledge of what we were facing, this was unreal, totally unreal. The weather was still cold so there wasn't the stench you might have experienced had it been warmer. But there was a smell of death – I'd smelt that during combat when we'd come upon the enemy – dead soldiers and horses and all that. And the odour was there, of death, mingled with the smell of the internees because they hadn't had a bath or a shower in forever.

I was totally unprepared for what I saw at Dachau – It was just beyond my imagination – like entering a nightmare. None of us – my battalion commander included – knew what was going on as we'd been heavily involved in combat against the enemy so we had no idea what some of that enemy was doing to Jews, Poles and other displaced persons. It was only many years later, on a visit to the memorial with my wife, that I learned that Dachau was also the very first concentration camp to incarcerate homosexuals and people who were against Hitler's movement. But at the time I had no knowledge of any of this.

I guess that seeing that train load of bodies was the first revulsion – I felt the bile coming up into my throat from seeing this. I couldn't understand what in the world had gone wrong here. I was a young lieutenant of twenty years and had never ever seen anything of this sort before. I'd seen death, of course, in combat, but you know, we're fighting an enemy and you expect to find dead people when you're shooting live rounds. But to find something like this – I just couldn't believe what I was seeing – I could not believe it. There were probably 15,000 dead bodies in Dachau alone and I imagine a similar number in Buchenwald, Bergen-Belsen and other camps. With all those bodies, we found only one live person on that train. One of the sergeants heard this moaning – I didn't see this personally but heard about it and there were photographs of it shown later.

I met this Belgian captain when I came through the gate. He had been captured only recently so he wasn't as badly off as some of them. He was a bit out of his head, I guess because of his experiences – seeing all this death. But he had been treated better, because he was an officer and, maybe because the Germans were thinking that as the war was nearing its end, they should take better care of this prisoner. Well, being Belgian, he spoke some English and I spoke German, so between us we were able to communicate with the prisoners. Although he hadn't been there long, he told me about the atrocious handling of prisoners and, that although he'd stayed as much as possible in the background, he knew what was going on. He told me that just before we had arrived there had been a lot of execution-style killings because of this letter that Heinrich Himmler had written to the commandants of all the camps saying there should be no survivors by the time the Allies arrived.

All the time I was there, I couldn't figure it out – why are all these people here? Why are so many dead? What did they do to deserve all this? Those were my thoughts. Not having any background knowledge, I couldn't understand what the Holocaust was – what is this cruelty from one human to another? I couldn't fathom it – it was overwhelming to all of us that went in there, even to hardened combat veterans, we'd never seen anything like this. Being a company commander I had to maintain control of my troops; my job was to lead them and tell them what to do and not go to pieces myself. I had an awfully hard time doing this – this was very different to death in combat. A lot of my guys had a terrible time with this, some of them fainted, some vomited. I felt like vomiting myself, but I couldn't let myself do that, since I was the leader of this group. And there was another difficulty: here I am, supposed to be a liberator but my orders were to keep all the inmates in the camp because if they had gotten out, they'd have died; they hadn't had enough food and could hardly walk, to say nothing of going out into the world again and fending for themselves – it would have killed them. But many of the prisoners who could speak a little broken English came and thanked me. They wanted to tell me about how they'd experienced this horror for so long and

then, all of a sudden, they had been given hope that they were going to survive – that's what they wanted to tell me. I couldn't communicate too well with them, but I think they knew – I felt that they knew we were there to save them. From that standpoint, I was very elated to think that we'd saved so many lives.

After the liberation, I had a great job as the information and education officer of our division, so I stayed there for a year before I came home. But I started having nightmares right away – for ten years after the war I had nightmares – horrific nightmares – and I couldn't stop thinking about how many of the guys had fainted or vomited; but I never talked about it – never. I was married right after I got back from overseas in 1946, and I never discussed it with my wife, so I didn't speak about it to her, to my children, to anybody. It was my second wife, Marge, who encouraged me to talk. And only then did it all come out and I figured that maybe now I was over it; but I wasn't. So, six years ago Marge and I went back to Europe, the purpose really being to traverse my Second World War combat trail. We went to Dachau, which is now a memorial, and all kinds of things came back to me. I remembered people pressing forward when they saw us coming – they'd forgotten that the fence was electrified and that if they touched it they'd be electrocuted, so many of them were impaled. I had completely forgotten about that, until, as we entered through the visitors' gate, I saw these insulators on the fence along the moat and, all of a sudden, this memory came flooding back and I just burst into tears. God Almighty, I remembered this happening and that, at the time, I was both a liberator and an executioner. And I still think about that and wonder, could we have gotten there earlier and saved more? Maybe if we had known what was going on in those camps, maybe we could have gotten there sooner. But we didn't know.

We had been driving all over Europe in a little Volkswagen and we arrived at the town of Dachau on the way down from Nuremberg. Before we found the camp we asked a couple of people of our age for directions but they said they didn't know where it was. And I felt like saying, 'The hell you don't know where it is.' I asked in German, 'Have you lived here in Dachau all your life?' 'Oh yes,' came the reply. So then I asked, still in German, 'Where is the concentration camp memorial?' and then I got this denial: 'I don't know what you're talking about.' Back in 1945, I remember, we had collected all the residents that we could find in the town and taken them into the camp; we had interviewed them and

asked them 'Did you know what was going on here?' *'Nein, nein'* – they didn't dare to know for fear they'd be in the camp themselves – they had all said. And when they got in there a lot of them had fainted and they just couldn't believe what they were seeing. We said 'How could you not know? The stench from the crematorium must have told you something was going on there; the trains in the middle of the night bringing dead bodies to the crematorium – how could you not know?' Again their defence was 'we didn't dare to even think that something like that was going on.' And yet, fifty years later, this same denial. In fact, I've run into people who say it never happened – never happened – and I'd say 'Oh yeah!' It very much did happen – to millions of people – Jews, Poles, Russians and many others – annihilated by a nation gone absolutely nuts – Nazi Germany. That's what I mean by the denial – I can't believe that so much denial existed then and still exists.

To this day I don't think the world has learned its lesson; so many atrocities are still being committed – in Bosnia, Herzegovina, Rwanda – all the killing and genocide, particularly in what was Yugoslavia. So, I would say the Holocaust didn't teach people anything; as long as there are human beings I think there will be some of this going on. Maybe not to the

Warren Dunn walks with his wife Marge in a veterans' cemetery, Los Angeles, California.

extent of Nazi Germany, but there's still thousands of people being persecuted and killed when a nation, or an element of a nation, thinks it's all powerful and can eliminate another population. As long as that happens, it's just going to go on forever. I have hope that perhaps with enough people talking about what happened in Nazi Germany, in Poland and other places in Europe – and what recently happened in Yugoslavia – maybe with enough people talking about it, bringing it to the forefront so that it's totally recognisable by everybody in the world – maybe then we'll finally come to grips with it and ensure that such atrocities can never be repeated.

I do still have a hard time forgiving the Germans – people of my own age – when I remember the children we found in the camp. And that's another reason why I have told my six children, four grandchildren and two great grandchildren what happened – maybe in my small way I can educate them about what transpired when I was a 20-year-old, and just maybe they'll grow up to prevent it happening again. I do have some hope for younger people and I feel wonderful that I was there and able to save so many – I just regret that I couldn't have gotten there sooner.

KATSUGO MIHO

Katsugo Miho, a liberator of the Dachau concentration camp. As he was liberating the camp, his father was being detained in an internment camp by the United States government.

I was born and raised on the island of Maui, Hawaii. On 7 December, when the Japanese bombed Pearl Harbor and the war broke out, leading members of the Japanese community were all picked up and, on the same night, my father was interned as an enemy of the state. He was a Japanese language-school teacher and they were all suspected of being agents for the Japanese government.

At that time I was at the University of Hawaii and on the morning of the 7th, all ROTC members were called into service. We all volunteered and served as members of the Hawaiian Territorial Guard. About a month and a half later a New York ranking officer took charge of security in Hawaii.

Inspecting the island of Oahu, he saw many Asian faces guarding the water pump and electrical stations and he found out that we were all Japanese-Americans. He became quite concerned and immediately

ordered the discharge of all Japanese-American members of the Hawaiian Territorial Guard.

I returned to Maui, qualified as a carpenter's apprentice, and went to work in a military air field, building barracks. In the meantime, the 100th Infantry Battalion, made up of mostly Hawaiian Nisei (Japanese-Americans) who were in the army prior to the war, were training in Wisconsin. The War Department decided that they would take a chance and the 100th was sent to Italy to join the 34th Infantry Division. In 1943 the 442nd Regimental Combat Team was formed and I volunteered for this all-Nisei military unit.

During my basic training at Camp Shelby we were given an opportunity to visit Camp Livingston, Louisiana, where my father was at the time. I had the chance to see him and and was shocked to find that he was being treated as a Prisoner of

War. I also had the chance to visit one of those Relocation Centers where thousands of Japanese-Americans from the west coast had been involuntarily located. The camp was surrounded by double barbed-wire fences and the four corners were guarded by manned machine-gun posts with guns pointing inside the camp. When we came to visit, although we were in American uniforms, we were searched by Caucasian American GIs with drawn weapons. The great majority of the people in the camp were women and children and American citizens. After our visits and protestations, life in the Relocation Centers improved.

When the 442nd Regimental Combat Team was sent overseas I participated in the battles in Italy and France and the 522nd Field Artillery Battalion was separated from the 442nd RCT and participated in the invasion of Germany and the battles of Mannheim, Frankfurt, Heidelberg, Ulm and were knocking on the steps of Berchesgarten when Germany surrendered. In late April we were in the vicinity of Munich and what we found out to be concentration camps. We later learned that Dachau, the main camp, had tens of thousands of inmates.

Our reconnaissance squad shot open the locks to one of the sub-camps and allowed thousands of inmates to get out. Starving, looking like the walking dead,

they began to roam the snow-covered countryside, just trying to find something to eat. The Germans had been using horses to cart their artillery and supplies, so there were a lot of dead horses lying along the roadsides. Against their better judgement, these inmates were stripping the horses and eating the flesh. Some of them died because they couldn't digest something like that. All of us gave whatever C-rations we had. C-rations were our emergency food supply and included things like hard biscuits, cheese and chocolates. Later, when we had had our chow, they would come to the vicinity of the chow line and beg for the leftovers. We gave them whatever was there and that's how, against orders not to feed them anything, we just could not resist doing whatever we could to ease the pain and suffering of these walking skeletons. I guess the fact that they were out of the camp was, in itself, enough to give them hope – they were no longer behind barbed-wire fences, they were free!

Many of the inmates were Ukrainian. That's my memory of who they were – Ukrainian Jews. They were wearing flannel pyjamas, that's all they had: blue-striped, white-striped flannel pyjamas. There was no need to exchange language because it was so obvious what they needed and we had so little to give. So there was very little communication – but we were able to communicate our concern and sympathy through our sign and body language, and we could see gratitude in their eyes; you could sense the flicker of hope and happiness when someone gives a helping hand.

In the meantime, whilst I was in and around Dachau, my Dad was still considered a Prisoner of War and was being interned in Santa Fe, New Mexico. Many members of the 442nd RCT throughout the war had parents, brothers and sisters in the so-called Relocation Centers throughout the United States.

I've seen many horrible sights in the two years I spent in Italy, France and Germany, but nothing prepared me for what we saw of the refugees from the concentration camps. We saw corpses of Germans and Americans on the battle fields, in all kinds of grotesque conditions, but the worst I've ever seen in my life were the survivors of the Holocaust – that is something I will never forget.

EPILOGUE

DR RANDOLPH BRAHAM

It is one of the tragedies of the Second World War that the Jews of Hungary were destroyed on the eve of Allied victory. Although subjected to discrimination that claimed close to 64,000 lives and violated basic civil rights, the bulk of Hungarian Jewry survived the majority of the war. Generally patriotic, the Jews were confident that what happened elsewhere in Nazi-dominated Europe could not happen in civilized Hungary.

In October 1942, a few high-ranking Hungarians secretly approached one of Eichmann's closest associates to discuss a "resettlement" programme beginning with 100,000 "Eastern" Jews inhabiting the northeast of Hungary. Aware of government opposition to the Nazi-style "solution", Eichmann preferred to wait for Hungarian consent to the "resettlement" of all Jews. Germany's occupation of Hungary on 19 March 1944 offered that opportunity.

The events that led to the occupation began shortly after the crushing defeat of the Hungarian and German armies at Voronezh and Stalingrad early in 1943. Realizing that the Axis had lost the war, the Kállay government became eager to extricate Hungary from the German alliance. Hitler knew of the Hungarians' "secret" negotiations with the Western Allies and resolved to frustrate their plans in order to protect the interests of the Reich, sealing the fate of Hungarian Jewry.

The occupation enabled the Nazis and their accomplices to implement the "Final Solution" at lightning speed. Time was of the essence. The Red Army was fast approaching Romania; the Western Allies were finalizing D-Day plans. World leaders, including national and Jewish leaders of Hungary, were already aware of the realities of Auschwitz. Excepting a few diehards, even the Nazis realized that the Axis had lost. Precisely because of this, the SS resolved to win the war against the Jews.

By this time in 1944, the Nazis' machinery of destruction was well tested. With experience gained through the mass murder of Jews all over German-dominated Europe, the Nazis were well able to handle a speedy operation in Hungary. They updated the death factories in Auschwitz and extended the rail lines leading to the immediate vicinity of the gas chambers in Birkenau. Within Hungary, the Eichmann *Sonderkommando*, consisting of relatively few SS "advisers", enjoyed the wholehearted support of the new Sztójay government.

Without that uneqivocal support the Nazis would have been helpless. The SS commando leaders were amazed by their Hungarian counterparts' enthusiasm for implementing the "Final Solution" program. The constitutionally appointed government placed the instruments of state power at the *Sonderkommando*'s disposal. With Horthy remaining at the helm, providing the façade of national sovereignty, the Hungarian police, gendarmerie, and civil service collaborated with the SS with a routine and brutal efficiency, often surpassing that of the Nazis themselves. From late March to mid-May 1944, they and their Nazi "advisers" completed the first phase of the anti-Jewish drive: the Jews were isolated, marked, expropriated, and placed in ghettos. During the next two months, the Jews were subjected to the most barbaric and speedy deportation and extermination programme, so massive that the crematoria in Auschwitz-Birkenau could not cope. Ditches had to be dug to burn the thousands of victims the crematoria could not. This last major campaign in the war against European Jewry involved the deportation of close to 440,000 Hungarian Jews. By the time the deportations were halted on 9 July – the day Wallenberg arrived on his mission of rescue – all of Hungary (with the exception of Budapest) was already *Judenrein* – free of Jews.

The magnitude of the catastrophe is illustrated by the following statistics. For example, on 6 June 1944 (D-Day), when the greatest multinational armada ever assembled under one command stormed the Normandy beaches, three transports arrived in Auschwitz-Birkenau with close to 12,000 Jews from Northern Transylvania. By the end of that day, the casualties of the Allies were about half of those suffered by the Hungarian Jews. Allied casualties declined sharply after they safeguarded the beaches, but the Jews continued to be murdered at the same rate day after day until 9 July. The military and civilian casualties of Britain –

a country that bore much of the German military onslaught – represented only half of the losses of Hungarian Jewry. These figures are cited not to minimize the sacrifices of the Western Allies, but to underscore the magnitude of the Holocaust in Hungary.

When Auschwitz was no longer feasible as an end destination because of the approaching Red Army late in 1944, thousands of Budapest Jews were forced to march toward the Reich. Many unshod, emaciated, underdressed prisoners died on the way, of starvation and typhoid fever; many more died in the camps along the border and in the camps in Germany itself: Mauthausen, Buchenwald, Bergen-Belsen.

Hungarian Jewry suffered close to 600,000 casualties, representing approximately 10 per cent of the wartime catastrophe of European Jewry. More than 10 per cent of the victims of the Hungarian chapter of the Holocaust consisted of labour servicemen. The labour service system was both unique and paradoxical. The paramilitary forced labour system for Jews of military age was introduced in 1939. Jewish recruits were assigned to work on roads, forest clearance and military infrastructure. After Hungary joined Nazi Germany's war against the Soviet Union in June 1941, the labour servicemen's lot changed for the worse:

they were compelled to provide their own clothes and wear armbands, making them easy targets for German, Hungarian, and other antisemites. Close to 50,000 labour servicemen deployed along the Soviet front were subjected to unimaginable cruelty. Thousands of others laboured in the Serbian copper mines in horrendous conditions. Their lot varied, depending on the guards and commanding officers.

The nemesis of Jews during the pre-occupation era, the labour service system emerged as a virtual haven after. Under direct Hungarian jurisdiction, the servicemen enjoyed the protection of the military authorities. Some decent company officers actually "recruited" Jews to save them from deportation. Their situation changed for the worse after the Arrow Cross Party coup of 15 October 1944. During the last few months of the war, thousands were deported to Nazi concentration camps where they shared the tragic fate of other Jews.

I myself am a survivor of the Hungarian Holocaust. On 4 October 1943, when I was drafted into forced labour service, I took leave of my parents with a normal good-bye, believing I would see them again – but I never did. I knew nothing of what happened to them until 1945 when my sister, Margaret, who had been liberated from a camp in northern Germany, returned and told me that, upon arrival in Auschwitz she and my parents had been separated: my parents ended up in the line destined for gassing.

I was liberated in January 1945 near the Hungary–Slovakian border. After a stint in a Soviet POW camp, I returned to my hometown in Transylvania and resumed my studies, but after a year of living in the devastation, I decided to join my relatives in the United States. With a Hillel fellowship I entered the City College of New York – an institution from which I retired as a faculty member in 1992.

It was during studies for my doctorate in political science that I developed a special interest in the Holocaust. In 1953–4, I became an associate of the YIVO-Institute for Jewish Research, working on biblio-graphical and documentary projects in conjunction with *Yad Vashem*, established that very year in Jerusalem. I was naturally attracted to finding answers to the enigma: how was it possible for the Nazis and their accomplices to make Hungary *Judenrein* on the eve of Allied victory, when the world was already acquainted with Auschwitz? I decided to seek answers using the tools of the social sciences, and to be as objective and as empirical as possible.

There is no chapter in human history as well documented as the Holocaust. Has the world learned the lesson of the Holocaust? The warning of George Santayana, the noted American philosopher, is still valid: the world must learn the lessons of the past in order to safeguard the future. When one thinks of the major catastrophes of the post-Holocaust era – mass murders in Uganda, the Sudan, Rwanda, Burundi, Cambodia, and the Balkans – one is inclined to conclude that the world has learned little. I strongly believe that the Holocaust has to be taught as a chapter in the long history of man's inhumanity to man. That history is replete with lessons about the devastating impact of intolerance, hatred, discrimination, and persecution. Clearly, one cannot ignore the suffering inflicted on people because of their race, colour or creed. It is generally assumed that the Holocaust is unique in the long history of man's inhumanity to man. For, in contrast to all other acts of genocide – horrendous acts perpetrated for the attainment of religious, ethnic or political objectives, the Holocaust represented the attempt of the Nazis and their accomplices to murder all Jews, irrespective of their age, sex or residence. The Holocaust must be taught as the possible culmination of the horror that can occur when man loses moral integrity and belief in the sanctity of human life. *The Last Days* is a potent and convincing contribution to this learning process.

THE SHOAH FOUNDATION

Some of the thousands of volunteers at work at the Shoah Foundation.

Cataloguers at work with Shoah Foundation-designed computer programs to index Holocaust survivor testimonies, allowing research by key word, name, place and other criteria.

Survivors of the Shoah Visual History Foundation was established by Steven Spielberg in 1994 with an urgent mission: to chronicle – before it was too late – the first-hand accounts of Holocaust survivors and witnesses, liberators and rescuers. With the goal of recording tens of thousands of eye-witness testimonies –

the largest undertaking of its kind – the Shoah Foundation assembled a multimedia archive to be used as an educational and research tool. The legacy of the Holocaust experiences of Jewish and non-Jewish witnesses endowed the collected archive with a rich diversity of perspectives and insights composed from the survivors of ghettos and camps; child survivors; refugees; members of the resistance including partisans, rescuers and aid providers; Jehovah's Witnesses; Sinti/Roma (Gypsy) survivors; homosexual survivors; survivors of eugenics policies; war crimes trials staff members and witnesses; liberators and liberation witnesses, as well as other eye witnesses.

The archive is comprised of more than 50,000 unedited testimonies – over 230,000 video tapes filled with over 115,000 hours of testimony. It would take

more than thirteen years to watch the collection from beginning to end.

The Foundation developed an in-depth indexing system capable of cataloguing the wide range of historical, biographical and geographical data offered by each witness. The catalogued testimonies form the backbone of the Foundation's Digital Library System, which allows researchers, educators and others to search through the archive from remote sites.

The entire archive will be made available to museums, educational institutions and other repositories for research and exhibition purposes. At the same time, the Foundation is using innovative ways of disseminating the collection to promote tolerance and cultural understanding worldwide. The Foundation has released an interactive educational CD-ROM, *Survivors: Testimonies of the Holocaust*, and two award-winning television documentaries: *Survivors of the Holocaust* and *The Lost Children of Berlin*. *The Last Days* is the Foundation's first feature-length documentary and the first to be released theatrically. Study guides have been developed for all of the Foundation's projects, providing teachers with effective tools to teach the history of the Holocaust and lessons of tolerance. The archive will also be available for use in the development of interactive travelling exhibits, and in the co-ordination of local and regional videotape libraries.

The dream of making this archive a reality was made possible by people throughout the world who dedicated themselves to this common goal. A culturally, ethnically, and religiously diverse group has come together – more than 3,500 interviewers, 1,000 videographers, 2,000 volunteers, 2,000 community leaders and individuals, and 240 staff members worldwide – bringing with them their collective knowledge, expertise, and experiences.

Soon the last eye witnesses to the Holocaust will be gone, but the work of the Shoah Foundation will enable people worldwide to see history through the accounts of tens of thousands of individuals who endured and survived it. It is a legacy that will benefit countless students, teachers, researchers and the public worldwide.

To contact the Shoah Foundation from the United States or Canada, telephone (818) 777-4673 or write to Survivors of the Shoah Visual History Foundation, PO Box 3168, Los Angeles, CA 90078 USA.

The transfer stations at the Shoah Foundation, where original video tapes of survivor interviews are duplicated: one protection copy, one cataloguing copy, one copy for the digital library and one copy to be sent to the survivor who gave the testimony.

SOURCES AND RECOMMENDATIONS FOR FURTHER READING

The definitive study on the Holocaust in Hungary is Randolph L. Braham, *The Politics of Genocide: The Holocaust in Hungary*, 2 vols (New York, 1981: revised edition 1994). Braham also compiled an invaluable, annotated collection of documents, *The Destruction of Hungarian Jewry: A Documentary Account*, 2 vols (New York, 1963; republished 1973).

The most accessible and reliable account of Hungarian Jewish history is Raphael Patai, *The Jews of Hungary. History, Culture, Psychology* (Detroit, 1996).

For a good, up-to-date introduction to the complexities of Hungarian history, see Peter Sugar, Peter Hanak, Tibor Frank (eds), *A History of Hungary* (London, 1990).

On antisemitism in Hungary, see Nathaniel Katzburg, *Hungary and the Jews 1920–1943* (Bar Ilan, 1981) and Moshe Y. Herczl, *Christianity and the Holocaust of Hungarian Jewry,* translated by Joel Lerner (New York, 1993). On resistance and rescue see Asher Cohen, *The Halutz Resistance in Hungary, 1942–1944* (New York, 1986), Arieh Ben-Tov, *Facing the Holocaust in Budapest. The International Committee of the Red Cross and the Jews in Hungary, 1943–1945* (Dordrecht, 1988) and Per Anger, *With Wallenberg in Budapest* (New York, 1981).

For a collection of essays exploring resistance and rescue in the Jewish and non-Jewish world see David Cesarani (ed), *Genocide and Rescue: The Holocaust in Hungary 1944* (Oxford, 1997).

Randolph L. Braham explores the post-war ramifications of the Holocaust in Hungary in 'Hungary', in David Wyman (ed), *The World Reacts to the Holocaust* (Baltimore, 1996), pp. 208–218, a volume that includes chapters, in which the reactions of Britain and the USA are ably summarised. Braham also edited three collections of essays, *The Holocaust in Hungary Forty Years Later* (New York, 1985), *The Tragedy of Hungarian Jewry* (New York, 1986) and *Studies on the Holocaust in Hungary* (New York, 1990) in which a range of scholars explore various aspects.

In addition to oral testimony the survivors created an astonishingly rich literature. The many works of Elie Wiesel are foremost, but the following illuminate the catastrophe from different standpoints with no less intensity: Hedi Fried, *The Road to Auschwitz: Fragments of a Life*, edited and translated by Michael Meyer (London, 1990); Isabella Leitner and Irving A Leitner, *Isabelle. From Auschwitz to Freedom* (New York, 1994) [part of which first appeared as *Fragments of Isabella* in 1978]; Ernö Szép, *The Smell of Humans*, translated by John Bátki (London, 1994); Trudi Levi, *A Cat Called Adolf* (London, 1995); Gerald Jacobs and Miklós Hammer, *Sacred Games* (London, 1995).